NOT THE SAME OLD SONG AND DANCE

The Wit and Wisdom of Peter Harvey Spencer

Compiled and Edited by Paul M. O'Rourke

WESTERN REFLECTIONS PUBLISHING COMPANY®

Montrose, Colorado

ISBN 1-932738-03-7

Library of Congress Control Number: 2004104406

Cover: *A man whose smile could light up a room, and whose laugh could bring down the house. Peter Spencer in attendance at the Jefferson Davis Memorial Brunch, October 1988.*
Photo by Ingrid Lundahl, ingridphoto@frontier.net

Cover and text design: Laurie Goralka Design

First Edition
Printed in the United States of America

Western Reflections Publishing Company®
219 Main Street
Montrose, CO 81401
www.westernreflectionspub.com

For Peter

Introduction

They were good Mondays. For just over two years — from May 1994 to August 1996 — every Monday was a special day. Mondays meant that *The Norwood Post* was going to be delivered to my home. It didn't matter that the paper had already been distributed to subscribers and boxes throughout southwestern Colorado the previous Wednesday. *The Norwood Post* was not just another paper, and it wasn't just "news" that made it special. It was Peter Spencer's newspaper, and his op-ed column, *Fearless Leader*, was what I looked forward to most. From one issue to the next, from one editorial topic to another, *The Post* and Peter's writing made my day, every Monday.

We were seated at the corner table in the Last Dollar in Telluride on a Sunday morning, during Film Week, in 1996. I was unaware that Peter was in the process of selling *The Norwood Post*, but it was obvious he had something weighing heavy on his mind. Between the several jokes told at the expense of the numerous passers-by who seemed more than slightly preoccupied by laminated festival passes that hung from their necks, Peter wanted to talk about writing, about *his* writing. He pulled a file folder from his well-traveled leather briefcase. It contained two of his editorials from *The Post*, his favorites he said.

"I want you to go through these," he insisted. "Liven them up, add where you need to. I want to get them — and several others — published."

"I like what I did better," was his straight-faced response some months later, after reading what I had "livened up." He was right, of course. You simply can't improve on an original, and Peter Spencer was nothing, if not original.

Peter created a website for some of his better writing efforts, but got no closer to bringing his work to an actual publisher. Following Peter's death in 1999, I sensed, immediately, what had to be done. As I transcribed one editorial after another onto my computer, I relived the excitement I felt when I got *The Norwood Post* on those Monday afternoons, and recalled our meeting at the Dollar, when he planted the idea of a published work firmly in my mind. *Not the Same Old Song and Dance* is Peter's work and his dream. I don't think he will be disappointed.

Editor

Foreword

Peter Spencer chose his words well, and, as many will attest, often. He so loved the language. For his friends he always had a kind word, an anecdote, a quote, a piece of historical trivia made poignant by the moment. A stroll down main street in Telluride with Peter required an abundance of spare time and an appreciation for topics ranging from the first buck taken during bow season to the lyrical poetry of Robert Burns. A consistent honesty marked every conference he conducted, for Peter was truly interested, if not wildly excited, in everything *he* had to say. You could see it in his eyes, and hear it in his laugh.

More than a storyteller, Peter was a thespian. Conversation for him was theater; each colloquy was carried out as though on the grand stage. When court was in session at the Sheridan or at the Dollar or at the Elks or on the street corner, Peter's eyes were a dead giveaway that a good story was on the verge of its telling. His eyes, those intensely intelligent, sparkling orbs, darted left, then right, then left again as though in a cerebral file search for some grain of wisdom, for some appropriately witty and little-known fact. He seldom missed the mark. His storehouse of information, of unusual stories and long forgotten quotes, was as endless as it was priceless.

Of course, there is precious little difference between good storytelling and writing. Yet, Peter didn't write simply because he wanted to say something, he wrote because he had something to say. Though he had to push himself, Peter went about the task of writing — often under the gun of an impending deadline — with a determined grace and a sense of humor. His style, when pen finally met paper, was light yet full of meaning. Peter's writings were like a much-needed vacation, a momentary escape from the daily grind. He lifted us up, made us feel good and at the same time counseled us to take a hard look at ourselves, and then gingerly put us back down with a chuckle. We marveled at how he could do so much with so few words.

Peter loved history, and writing about events and places and people found only in the deep recesses of the collective memory. For a man who was "ahead of his time" — an avowed computer geek — his love of the past may seem slightly inimical. Yet, Peter Spencer was a man of many sides — he wore more hats than Imelda wore shoes. For Peter, history was a large storehouse of facts and personalities from which a lively story might be spun, its potential much like the infiniteness of software application. History and computers were vehicles for Peter, a means of transportation on the boundless path of learning. Peter was always the student. That is why he was such a good teacher.

Peter's attraction to journalism surprised absolutely no one. His instinctual curiosity and his appetite for information made him a natural — his love of the language didn't hurt, either. According to Ernest Hemingway, the essence of the "writer as journalist" is the ability to meaningfully express "the good and the bad, the ecstasy, the remorse and sorrow, the people and the places, and how the weather was." Peter had a wonderful sense for and empathy with his surroundings and his neighbors, and he knew which way the wind blew.

Peter's editorials in *The Norwood Post* were personal letters to his readers, their strength and appeal made apparent by the volumes of correspondence he received in the return mail. He loved a good story and found great joy in its telling, especially if it was just ever so slightly controversial. Peter's "opinions" were meant to stir the pot, to get people talking. They were an invitation to dialogue. After all, Peter loved nothing better than people talking, especially if he was at the center of the conversation.

When Peter successfully ran for mayor of Telluride, his campaign slogan proclaimed, "Not the Same Old Song and Dance." I can't think of a better way to explain who Peter Spencer was as a politician, who Peter Spencer was as a journalist and writer, and who Peter Spencer was as a human being. This book is a tribute to what he saw and felt and so eloquently put to words. It is, as he was, *Not the Same Old Song and Dance.*

Paul O'Rourke

Acknowledgements

The compiler and editor of this book extends his appreciation and affection to Peter's family. For lending their encouragement to this project and approving the publication of Peter's work, I am truly grateful.

The compiler acknowledges *The Norwood Post,* the original publisher of Peter's editorials. Past issues of *The Norwood Post* are available to the public thanks to the Wilkinson Library in Telluride, the Colorado Historical Society Library in Denver, and the Norwood Public Library.

To Bonnie Beach, who expertly and thoughtfully provided editorial clarity and consistency to the text — not to mention a few needed commas and periods — many thanks are due.

For their heartfelt reminiscences and inspirations, thank you to Roudy Roudebush, Bob Beer, Leslie Sherlock, Randy Sublett, Glenn Herbert, Bobbie Shaffer, Mary Duffy, and Judi Kiernan.

For their technical and very artistic wizardry, the editor wishes to acknowledge photographer Steve Larson as well as Tor Anderson, Art Director at Telluride Publishing.

Not the Same Old Song and Dance was produced in cooperation with the Telluride Council for the Arts and Humanities, thanks in part to grants from the Telluride Commission on the Arts and Special Events and San Miguel County.

Elegy for Peter

What will the words do now that you are gone?
The verbs you once wrestled into prose will grow rusty
The nouns you once teased into play shall gather dust
Unborn puns will return to slumber
Unread poems will mourn your voice
Punch lines will forget themselves

In the gray that shrouds this day after your death
The dictionary weeps
The blank pages sob
There's a silence no language can break
A silence that swarms in our bones
What will the words do without you?

Rosemerry Wahtola Trommer

Contents

CHAPTER TWO
On Journalism...the First Draft of History

CHAPTER THREE
A Few Modest Proposals for Reform...or Jousting at
Bureaucratic Windmills

CHAPTER FOUR
Thoughts from an Oxygen-Deprived Mind...or I Just Checked In to See What Condition My Condition Was In

CHAPTER FIVE
A History Lesson...from a Fearless Perspective...or Stories from a Checkered Past

CHAPTER SIX
A View from the Canyon...Wayward Politics and the Environment

CHAPTER SEVEN
Teach Your Children Well...in the Techno-Age

EPILOGUE...STOP THE PRESSES

CHAPTER ONE

The Department of Local Affairs . . . or Life Sixty-five Miles from the Nearest Stop Light (at least until recently)

Preliminaries . . .

Peter Spencer was (and still is) a fan of mine. He was also a fan of bankers and lawyers and realtors and the boys at the Dollar who could carry on an animated conversation. While his written words are his legacy to us, I treasure our laughter-accented conversations most. God, we were witty, intelligent, confident barflies. We spoke at great length about issues of great interest but probably of questionable importance. Like myself, Peter the Showman always tried his act out at the Sheridan before committing it to print. During his sojourn as the "Quintessential Mayor" of Telluride, we shamelessly competed for national press coverage. As the "Quintessential Cowboy" I think I got the most press, but it was the horses who were really the stars. I just happened to be sitting on them.

Peter came to Telluride with a small fortune. He spent it, of course. Once, conversing in front of the courthouse (the Sheridan wasn't open yet), I said, "Let's get away from the back of this stinking diesel bus." And he said, "No, I like it. It reminds me of home. It's New York!" With Peter, place was more important than position, anyway. He made me appreciate New York in ways I'd never considered. He made me appreciate where and how I lived in ways I'd never considered.

Peter was a scammer's scammer. He lent an air of legality to our lifestyle here. His Jewish and my Irish mother had much in common. They instilled in us a healthy guilt about shirking our responsibility to "Save the World." We often commiserated that, having failed to save the "whole" world, perhaps we could save our small part of it.

I am a fan of Peter Spencer's. I try to live and talk and act in a manner he would approve of. I try to make informed decisions when I vote and continue my education so as to surprise the interviewers with the fact that isolation from the real world does not mean we don't think. I believe in many of the same things Peter did. I miss him sorely and daily. It was a better world when he was with us. As you read what he wrote, picture him in the Sheridan practicing his timing on a willing audience of cowboys and tourists and realtors and governors, regaling one and all with his booming laughter, filling in the muddy breaks.

— *Roudy Roudebush*

Adventure is Where You Find It

When you live 65 miles from the nearest traffic light and stay close to home for too many weeks, you find yourself yearning for the culinary delights of fast food and the heady excitement of chain stores. Those who live in the outside world may find it difficult to believe that we willingly undertake a three-hour round trip to McDonald's or Wendy's and anxiously look forward to spending a Saturday afternoon in Wal-Mart.

Having stayed somewhere between Silverton and Paradox for nearly three months and noticing that without an act of congress gas prices had moderated from their summer high, I filled the bottomless tank of my ancient Oldsmobile, brushed off the crushed velour seats, cleaned the moon roof, and headed over Dallas Divide for the wonders of Montrose and beyond. Ready for adventure, I cruised the blue bomb through Montrose without stopping and drove north toward the siren call of Grand Junction.

Stopping to refuel at Delta — they didn't worry about gas prices when they built the blue bomb — I savored my first taste of civilization with a three-piece dinner (original recipe) at the KFC and continued north with a growing sense of excitement.

Grand Junction is not on anyone's list of the ten most interesting cities in America. It lacks some of the charm of San Francisco, the culture and sophistication of New York, the earthy delights of New Orleans and the glitter of Las Vegas. But Grand Junction does have its compensations. It has a K-Mart and a Wal-Mart and a Target and a good Chinese restaurant, and most of all it has a Sam's Club. Deciding to go for the gusto, I drove straight for the Sam's Club.

I didn't really need anything, but then again if these marvels of modern distribution had to rely on people only buying what they needed, they would all soon follow the five and dime into extinction. I was looking forward to the expression on my five-pound cat's face when he realized how much I had saved on the hundred-pound bag of generic dry cat food.

Finally I reached the front of the line. The crowds had been building during the wait and the clerk asked for my membership card. I dusted off my wallet and proudly handed him my Sam's Club Card, complete with photo ID. He looked at my card, pulled himself up to his full height and announced that my card had expired.

"You can renew it right over there," he said, gesturing towards another 500 expectant people milling around a counter that looked for all the world like the driver's license examiner's office.

Still calm, I said, "Look, I'm paying cash. I have a long drive home and besides my cat is hungry. I'll renew it next time I come in."

"I will not take your money without a valid card," he said officiously.

Being normally soft spoken and reticent, my next action was totally out of character. I jumped up on the counter and in a voice that filled the cavernous emporium I shouted, "If Sam Walton were still alive he would have taken my money."

My shout struck a responsive chord and the huddled masses around the checkout took up the refrain.

"Bring back Sam," they began to chant. Soon the long lines around the membership counter joined the refrain and the clerk began to move backwards towards the door. Staff rallied to the threat and within minutes Godzilla the manager and her equally impressive tag team partner helped me down from the counter.

"We will be happy to take your money and help you check out," they said in unison.

Their check out speed was near record time and they thoughtfully carried all of my purchases to the car. After they helped me into the car with my purchases, the manager handed me a renewal application through the window.

"You can mail this in if you don't want to come back and wait in line," she said calmly.

I did.

I still haven't received my new card.

I think when I run out of Teriyaki sauce I am going to try a trip to Cortez.

September 25, 1996

⋆⇒◎⇐⋆

Changing Light Bulbs and Remembering Thomas Jefferson

Two new members were appointed to the San Miguel County Planning and Zoning Commission. They both have Telluride addresses. That leaves only one member of a commission that serves a 3,000-square-mile county living outside the Telluride region. What does that have to do with light bulbs and Jefferson? First a story, then the answer.

Back in another life when I was Mayor of Telluride, I was asked to speak at a meeting of the Montrose Rotary Club. Never one to miss an opportunity to be on stage, I accepted. The Montrose Rotary is very active and the luncheon meeting was attended by over two hundred people.

Montrose's business leaders had, and probably still have, a love/hate relationship with Telluride. They were well aware of the positive impact that Telluride's explosive growth was then having on the Montrose economy. They were also well aware of Telluride's old reputation for wild living. There was a feeling that the liberal political activism of Telluride was fueled by busybodies minding other people's business. Although the new Telluride was on the Western Slope, the vast majority at the meeting felt it was not of the Western Slope. There were a few friendly faces as I worked the crowd before we sat down to lunch: Montrose's extraordinary Mayor, Tricia Dickenson, Kelvin Kent from Montrose Decorating, and the brilliant attorney from Ouray, Chris Johnson. But there was no doubt in my mind that the rest were hostile. I took the podium at the Pavilion after lunch to polite, but unenthusiastic, applause. Looking at the set stares of the crowd, I was hoping that they had eaten all their salads and there were no tomatoes left to throw. We did establish a certain rapport, but that's another story.

One of the first rules of speech making is: if in doubt, tell a joke. Make sure it isn't sexist, racist or racy, and hope they haven't heard it before.

"How do you change a light bulb in Telluride?" I began. Before we get to the punch line, let us get back to planning and zoning.

At the San Miguel County Commission meeting last week, the commissioners appointed two new members to the seven member Planning and Zoning Commission. Henry Dusenbury of Norwood and Tom Smith of Telluride had both resigned, leaving two vacancies. Three Norwood residents had applied for a seat. As each of the four openings came up, Commissioner Leslie Sherlock argued that some balance should be maintained and one of the seats should be a Norwood appointment. Commissioners Anna Zivian and Jim Craft were unconvinced. They said that with the new growth management plan for the Telluride region being addressed this year, they wanted the commission to have a Telluride perspective. They appointed Telluride attorney Mick Obrand and environmental activist Poncho Winter to the commission, and reappointed Vern Ebert and Jane Conlin. That leaves Buddy Davis of Redvale as the only P & Z member west of Keystone Hill.

With the recent incorporation of the Mountain Village and the Town of Telluride moving to annex everything in sight, county planning activity in the Telluride region will be reduced, not increased, in the coming year. Planning issues are heating up on Wright's Mesa. We have to wonder if the new commission will bring a Telluride point of view to the agricultural lands of the mesa.

Jefferson warned that in a democracy we should fear a dictatorship of the majority. The rights of the minority must be protected. As the population continues to grow in the resort corner of the county, the commission must protect the essential balance between the new resort service economy and the traditional agricultural and light industrial economy of the rest of the county. Otherwise the only jobs left will be commuting to Telluride. Commissioners Zivian and Craft did not represent the entire county when they made their decision. They did Telluride a disservice as well by not bringing the Wright's Mesa perspective to planning. After all, you can see the horizon from here.

We did promise the rest of the story.

"How do you change a light bulb in Telluride?"

You hold it over your head and wait for the rest of the world to turn around you.

April 12, 1995

Why the Weather Man always Stands in Front of Norwood on the Map and Other Myths of Western Slope Weather Forecasting

In the winter the tourists generally ask, "Is it going to snow?"

The answer, of course, is "YES." It will, but when? Here on Wright's Mesa, if it is spring, it's generally safe to assume it's going to be windy. If it's Rodeo weekend, it will probably rain. If it's early January, my pipes will probably freeze and if we're planning a barbecue, there's an 80 percent chance of afternoon and evening thundershowers.

I think that the two Grand Junction TV stations are bush leagues for weather forecasters. If you can point at a map without falling down and pronounce Olathe correctly, you've got the job. Then, if you do well, you can move up to Pueblo or even Colorado Springs. If you do poorly you can run for office. (Mayor Theobold of GJ used to do the sports on Channel 8.) I sometimes catch Accuweather on the radio, and they are very good at reporting what the temperature was, in Montrose and Telluride, but I think people know that already.

If I lived where you could get cable, I could watch the Denver stations, but their weather forecasters don't know there's a Western Slope. They start at the Four Corners then jump to the mountains (read: Aspen) and then on to the Front Range. Ah, if only I could get NBC and watch Willard Scott. No weather-wanna-be is Willard, he trained for the job. Willard was the original Ronald MacDonald [sic]. It doesn't get much better than that. But alas, Willard stands in front of Norwood, too. "Here's the storm in the Pacific," standing in front of Norwood. Turning, but still blocking Norwood, "and here's the storm over Kansas, and the ice in the Northeast." The same goes for CNN and even the Weather Channel.

Why do they all cover up our forecast? Is it a plot? Then the answer struck me, "Only fools and flatlanders try to predict the weather in *Norwood Post* Country.

Being neither a fool nor a flatlander, today *The Norwood Post* introduces "do-it-yourself" weather forecasting. Through the miracle of modern digital electronics, we download Tuesday afternoon's last visual satellite picture of the western U.S. from the weather computers at the University of Illinois. We will publish these each week so you can figure out for yourself what's coming. You'll notice we're not standing in front of the map.

May 18, 1994

⋆⇒◯⇐⋆

What do Wynona, Madonna, Cher and Telluride Have in Common?

In the late seventies my wife and I arrived in Denver from North Carolina on a quest to find a small town in the mountains to make our home and get in some good skiing during the search. Before we left the South, we made a list of towns to check out and someone had mentioned Telluride, so we dutifully added it to the bottom of the list. For some unremembered reason, or perhaps just by chance, we decided to look there first. We asked everyone we met in Denver how to get to Telluride. No one could tell us. Answers ranged from "I think it's in Utah" to "How do you spell that?" "Never heard of it" was the most frequent. We finally tried Mountain Bell Information (that was US West before they stopped servicing telephones and became a conglomerate). Colorado only had one area code then, and the information operator was able to find the listing. "Whose number do you want?" she asked in the standard operator's monotone.

"Central Reservations," we said hopefully.

"I am sorry sir, there is no listing for Central Reservations."

"How about the Chamber of Commerce?" we asked a little less hopefully.

"We have no listing, and you only get one more try on this call."

"They must have a hotel or a lodge," we said, ready to start looking in Utah.

She must have taken pity on us and gave us two numbers, one for the New Sheridan Hotel and one for the Telluride Lodge. The New Sheridan didn't answer. We learned later that they rarely did answer the phone in those days. The Lodge answered and gave us directions through South Park and Buena Vista and Salida and Gunnison and Montrose and Ridgway to Telluride. Never having seen this part of the country before, we thought that seeing the breathtaking expanse of South Park after cresting Kenosha Pass was the most beautiful sight in America. We feel that way now as Wright's Mesa spreads out before us at the top of Norwood Hill.

It was late December and when we got to Telluride there was a pile of snow in the middle of the main street nearly eight feet high. The town didn't haul off the snow in those days. We never got to see the rest of the list. We bought a house in town (there wasn't a house over $100,000 and lots were selling for $10,000). We left only once the next year and that was to ship our furniture.

Every one we knew asked where we were moving. "Telluride, Colorado," we would tell them excitedly.

"Is that near Denver?" they would reply doubtfully.

"No, it's near Montrose," we would tell them.

"Montrose?"

"Well, Montrose is close to Grand Junction."

"Oh," they would say, unconvincingly. "Grand Junction, that's close to Denver?"

We finally learned to routinely say that we lived in Telluride, and it is 350 miles west of Denver, near the Utah border.

In those days you could go into Rose's at the corner of Aspen and Colorado and find Lael pricing canned goods and Dave Senior cutting meat. It wasn't long before you knew everyone at the Sheridan and the Roma and the Dollar and the Senate. If you stayed too late and overindulged, Hank Smith, the Town Marshal, would walk you home. Everyone in town needed from three to five jobs to make ends meet, but all the businesses and shops closed on powder days and there was plenty of time to ski. After freezing through five lift rides to get one run on the face, you would see the "Do Not Ski Alone" sign at Joint Point, and the ride was forgotten as you plunged into the unknown.

In the winter the ancient furnace in the County Courthouse belched black smoke every morning and in the summer the dust from the tailings pile created great gray clouds over the town.

Cars parked diagonally on the main street and before the Blue Bird buses started belching diesel fumes, Howard Linscott's horse teams pulled wagons and sleighs to get the skiers around town.

George Kovich was building stone walls. Tom John held court in the badly listing San Juan Baths; Tom Goldsmith cranked up the steam at the Boiler Room; the food co-op was under the Opera House; Howie was at the door of the Floradora every day at lunch; Jerry Vass would close the real estate office and roller skate down main street and Jim Bedford would introduce the movies at the Opera House. Wendy McFadden was cooking great breakfasts at the Sheridan; and the Iron Ladle, the Upper Crust and the Flour Garden could start your day right. Sherry Bruer was making donuts in her shop on Fat Alley. John Micetic was making great steaks at the Silverjack. The Ice House was a restaurant and Brewster and Carol served strawberry Daiquiris on the deck for Sunday Brunch. The Hopkins brothers were in the kitchen of the Powder House, and all your friends were waiting tables. And Monica was making an incredible cold peach soup at the Senate.

Jim Russel was running the Sheridan Bar where Walter McClennan held court every night. You could generally count on the Epoxy Sisters to show up at the Roma in drag and Primo won the Miss Telluride Contest. Every St. Patrick's Day Wacky Jack would ski down the face of the mountain wearing nothing but painted shamrocks. And it wasn't New Year's Day if you didn't show up at Hadley's for breakfast. Ron and Joyce threw great Christmas parties and gave Benchmark Bourbon for presents.

You knew every DJ on KOTO and they knew you. The Buzzards Ball didn't raise much money, but everyone went and usually dressed as their favorite local. The Gin Festival was still a secret and no one told a stranger how to find Dunton. They never had to ask your box number at the Post Office and there were counter checks in all the stores in case you forgot your checkbook.

In off-season, everything closed. There wasn't a restaurant or lodge open. If some hapless tourist showed up in late April, one of the few remaining residents would generally have to take them home for supper. The whole population was in Mexico or at Lake Powell.

We've noticed in national newspapers of late, Telluride is getting a lot of press. They don't say Telluride, Colorado anymore, just Telluride. Just as Wynona has joined Madonna and Cher in needing no additional identification, Telluride has joined Aspen and Vail in the rarefied atmosphere of instant recognition. People come to town with jobs and resumes. A lot has changed in Telluride since its rise to single name fame. Much of what has changed is not apparent to the locals of two- or even five-year tenure. There is so much that has been lost, and still much left that is worth preserving. Jerry Vass doesn't roller skate down Colorado Avenue anymore, and off-season is an endangered species.

We called the press office at the new Denver Airport Monday to get information for our article about their opening. "We're *The Norwood Post*, in Norwood, Colorado," we said.

"Where's Norwood?" they asked. They would have located us instantly if we told them we were near Telluride.

"Oh, we're about ten miles west of Redvale," we said. We hope to keep it that way.

March 1, 1995

⟶⟡⟵

The Law of Boom and Bust has Not Been Repealed. Ignore It at Your Peril.

Why is the memory so short when it comes to the boom and bust cycle? In another life, I was in the textile business in North Carolina. There was a rule in the fashion end of the business that every fashion trend was one year coming-in, one year in, and one year going-out. It was a good rule, but largely ignored. Large factories would get geared up to make vast quantities of last year's hot product, only to become large empty factories the next year. I am not in the textile business anymore because I built a huge manufacturing plant to make polyester double-knits. The plant came on line at the same time as K-Mart started selling them at 40 percent off.

The electronics business drives much of the economy today. The rule of electronics is "five years in the making, one year in the being." New product development that runs behind the competition misses the boom altogether and goes straight from coming-in to going-out.

Our part of the West is no stranger to the boom and bust cycle. Both in agriculture and mining, the cycles have proved more enduring than towns, mines, jobs and schemes. We wrote about the disappearance of the great sheep flocks of not too many years ago. In *Norwood Post* Country, the mining boomtowns of Uravan, Slick Rock, Alta, Tomboy and others that we've forgotten stand as mute evidence to the inevitability of the cycle.

Ranching has endured, but the number of ranches and cattle on the great mesas of San Miguel and Montrose Counties is far below the numbers of even 20 years ago. Placerville was once the largest cattle shipping point in the western United States.

Telluride and San Miguel County are devoting a lot of time to discussions of growth management. Attempting to manage the boom is a new concept. The population of Telluride and San Miguel County was larger in 1895 than it is today. Telluride had an estimated population of 5,000 at the turn of the century. That is more than the entire county today. There was no talk of growth management then. The petering out of the rich gold veins, the discovery of deposits in other parts of the world took care of the growth management.

The radium demand of the twenties kept the mines going in the west end of the counties. The Second World War and Atomic Energy Commission in the fifties kept things hopping. The discoveries of pitchblende ore in Africa and the disenchantment with nuclear [power] generation in America managed that boom down to zero.

What about the boom of tourism and giant second homes now overheating a real estate-driven economy? Will it go on forever? Will every mesa have its own subdivision? Is there no end? Take heart! Someday the city folk will find the next place to sink their excess income. Boom and Bust has not been repealed. Land that is no longer productive will eventually go back to nature. Make plans now for the inevitable bust.

I have a plan. I am going to build some benches in the back of the pick-up, put a canvas top over them and take guided tours of ghost subdivisions. I'll bet the tour demand never ends.

July 27, 1994

⊷⟶◉⟵⊶

The Bike Path May only Cost Two Million, but Can We Afford the Bike?

We've got a shiny new Chevy pick-up that we'll be making payments on until Volume 5, Number 26 of this paper. My wife lets me drive it sometimes, but I have to do the dishes and make the bed for a week. Generally I drive the Green Hornet, a wrinkled '72 Ford Ltd., bought last year for $400 from Jeannie Beer. It brings back fond memories of drive-ins and 25 cent a gallon gas. Before I got this job closer-to-home, I commuted every day to Telluride. With a satisfying surge of eight-cylinder power, the Hornet took me up and down Norwood and Keystone hills to work.

Now after the Telluride council buys the highway and builds the bike path and intercept parking, I suppose you'll need a permit to get into town. I guess the permits will go to the people who live in town and walk to work anyway.

When all that's done, and I deliver the papers on Wednesdays, I won't mind leaving the Hornet out at Society Turn and biking on in. That car is a bear to park anyway, and I sure need the exercise.

With some excitement, I started pricing mountain bikes. I found one for $1,600, but it didn't have the latest molybdenum frame and only came in pastel colors. I needed more. A man must have some pride in his machine after all.

I wonder if they could create a fund with the savings from government construction of the path and make low-interest bike loans to struggling commuters like me.

May 11, 1994

⊷⟶◉⟵⊶

Not in My Backyard, but Maybe in that Backyard Over There

A new jail in Norwood, great idea. The approximately 40-prisoner facility would create jobs during and after construction. A million dollar project certainly boosts the economy. Long term, an estimated 20 employees would staff the jail. That many jobs look good to a town with less than 350 people over the age of 16. Many of us spend two hours a day on increasingly crowded highways, climbing the hills to and from work. West End commuters, less than half way to work when they pass Norwood, could get jobs closer to home. Sheriff's officers would no longer spend two hours late at night with only a belligerent drunk for company, crossing Dallas Divide. The many extra trips for arraignments and trials could be eliminated. An annex for the criminal court located at the jail, or the use of video arraignments could save even more time and money. Not to mention all the ads we could run for bail bondsmen. Great idea. It's logical.

I eagerly went home to explain this newfound prosperity with my wife.

"Where are they going to put it?" she asked in her softest voice.

"Next to the county building is the logical place," I said in my most logical voice.

"The county building? You mean the one that's a block from the school where your nine-year old goes? The one that's across from the Quonset hut where she goes to dog club? The one that's next to the 4-H?"

"That's the one. What do you think?"

"I'll throw my body in front of the bulldozer!"

I wasn't winning this conversation so I talked about the unknown costs of the new jail in Montrose. If we don't build our own, we could be stuck with a big bill. If we don't build our own, we are exporting more jobs. If we don't build our own . . .

But it always came back to the same question. Where?

I tried to think of a place that wasn't close to school, that wasn't close to my house, that wasn't close to my friends' houses, that wasn't close to the houses of anyone I knew. A place we wouldn't have to drive by too often. When I got as far away as Red Mountain Pass, I stopped thinking.

If the jail project moves forward, the public will vote on it in November. We've got time to get all the facts and figures. I believe that the arguments for building a jail in Norwood will be compelling and I'm sure one of us can think of a place to put it.

May 4, 1994

---*≈◯═*---

They Never Built a Statue to a Critic

There is a lot to be done in the world. As long as we insist on locking up more and more people that commit crimes for longer and longer periods of time, one of the those things that have to be done is to build more jails to house them. It is a shame to spend so much public money on housing prisoners when so many more positive things could be done with the money, but there seems to be little alternative. Colorado statutes require all counties over 2,000 people to have county jails. San Miguel is the only Colorado county above 2,000 that does not have its own jail.

Sending prisoners to Montrose has not been a viable solution. The rising costs of housing prisoners in Montrose, combined with Montrose County's insistence that the cost contributions be open ended and with minimum guarantees of annual cell rental, make the alternative uncertain and expensive. Sending officers of a thinly spread county Sheriff's Department out of the county on an average 130-mile round trip to transport prisoners over roads that are often slowed to a crawl by severe winter weather and increasing traffic demands is not the best use of our law enforcement resources, and it is expensive. The county needs to build a jail. That is the easy part. The harder part is where.

The San Miguel County Commissioners and the Sheriff, after over a year of meetings and hearings and consultant's studies, unanimously chose the Summit Street site in Norwood. The issue was before the County Planning and Zoning Commission, the Norwood Planning and Zoning Commission, and the Norwood Town Board, and the zoning went to referendum. All concurred on the site: it was next to the current County facility and dispatch; most sheriff's officers live in the area; the County owned the land; water and sewer were available; and the consultant's studies showed the total cost to be the lowest of the seven sites studied. There also were strenuous objections from neighbors to some of the other potential sites.

The people who made the decision are our neighbors. There were elected officials, there were the volunteers who sit on the boards and there were the people who voted in the referendum. These are people who care about the safety of children as much as any of us. They did not see a special danger in the school being a block from the new jail.

Now a group of our neighbors have asked that the decision be reconsidered. They believe that there is great danger to the school children from a county jail. Some have threatened a mass recall. Others extended lawsuits. It isn't easy making the hard decisions. We hope that the safety concerns of these neighbors can be answered without an extended and expensive battle. There needs to be good will and a respect for all opinions on all sides of an issue in order to have a meaningful dialogue and answer concerns.

We do not share their concern, but we believe it to be genuine. We are much more concerned about the abusers that are not in jail than we are about the ones that are on the inside. It is a county jail, not a state prison. The bulk of the prisoners will be DUIs, bad checks and bar fights. We are surprised that there have been no objections to the Sheriff's work gangs, which we wrote about last month working outdoors at the fairgrounds, next to the 4-H barn and less than a block from the school.

We do have some concerns for our children. We are concerned that with reduced emergency medical services in the western parts of San Miguel and Montrose Counties that Norwood only has one ambulance equipped for critical transport to Montrose. The EMTs have been trying to raise $15,000 to equip the other ambulance properly. Thus far, the results, with the exception of Jim and Gretchen Wells' generous contribution and Ann Shaffer's hard work, have been disappointing at best. We would like to see some of the zeal that has been forthcoming protecting our children from the jail applied to equipping ambulances that can help the children in a medical emergency.

We have written about the need for extensive repair or rebuilding at the school. It needs to be carefully planned, options explored and a bond issue must be put before the electorate. We hope that the school board does not have its attention so diverted by the jail issue that it does not take the time to protect our children from an outdated, inadequate facility in need of extensive remediation.

We need to look for more activities for our children that are positive. We need to create a good place for them to congregate when they are not in school and not at home. A youth activities center should be high on the list of our priorities.

Little will be accomplished if the jail issue descends into an endless series of acrimonious meetings, lawsuits and the accompanying bitterness, and lack of final resolution. It needs to be settled now.

September 6, 1995

⊷═◉═⊷

The Best Laid Plans . . . a Cautionary Tale for Planners

Sometimes things don't work out the way we planned. It isn't Murphy's Law — it is The Law of Unintended Consequences. Problem solving can many times create worse problems.

The 1994 population estimate for San Miguel County is nearly 4,800 people. That is an increase of 31 percent since 1990. Worried about growth and change, the county and the Town of Telluride have funded a $200,000 study to come up with a Regional Growth Management Plan. Consultants have been hired, community input is being requested and meetings are being scheduled. A new vocabulary is being developed. Terms like Carrying Capacity are being bandied about. We think that means how many people can live in an area without destroying it. The process is supposed to take a year. Process is like Wonder Bread. It may taste pretty good, but enough of it will kill you.

We hope the planners get it right this time. We have had some experience with planning, and we didn't get it right. Maybe they can learn from our mistakes. Back in the '70s when we came to San Miguel County, we came because it was a beautiful place and we wanted to live here. Many others came for the same reasons. There seemed to be only two problems. The first, making a living here so we could stay, and the second was not messing things up. In some ways they became conflicting goals.

The first process started 20 years ago. To keep from messing things up, a regional growth plan was developed. There was a great concern about traffic increases and cars and parking in the Town of Telluride. Believing that the big land owners would like to have high-density compact developments, and that those developments would leave a lot of the open space untouched and that the market wanted to buy condominiums in those developments, we planned for that type of development. We put regulations on high-density development. They had to have alternative public transportation: trains, gondolas or other high-cost methods. We required public land dedications, impact mitigations, employee housing and an extensive review process. We knew that when the area was built out that there wouldn't be traffic problems because we could whiz the tourists to and from the town and the ski area without a tire ever touching the road. We weren't going to rely on smelly buses or dusty cars. We would have a compact pedestrian village on the ski mountain. Tourists wouldn't ever have to rent a car.

What happened?

The plan itself caused much of the problem. By putting expensive requirements on compact, dense development, only the largest and best-financed developers could consider that type of project. When the gondola is finally completed, the Mountain Village will be the only project that will have off-road transportation. It will certainly help, but it is doubtful that many of the homeowners scattered over the area will take advantage of the ride. Most other developers, unable to spend the millions necessary for a gondola or a train, opted for single-family homes. Market conditions favored homes over condos, and thus there has been a spread of large homes on large lots, eating the magnificent mesas of the whole county.

The traffic and cars are overwhelming. Seventy per cent of the working population of Norwood commutes to Telluride. When Highway 145 was closed Monday morning by a mudslide, we called the county officers to ask a question. The county attorney answered the phone; no one else could get to work. They all commute. The traffic count at Society Turn going on to the Telluride spur is nearly 8,000 per day. Five years ago it was less than 3,000. Back when the first plan was made, the cartoon character Pogo said, "We have met the enemy and they is us." It wasn't the tourists that created a car problem — it turned out to be all of us who live and work here. With all of the rules now being planned to keep the cars out of the east end of the county and expensive intercept parking being developed, no one seems to be interested in a county-wide bus system that would give immediate relief to the traffic and parking problems and would give a break to weary commuters.

We succeeded in improving the economy in the Telluride region. We wanted to do that so we could afford to stay here. That goal was also a victim of the Law of Unintended Consequences. Most of the people who were in Telluride in the '70s can't afford to live there anymore. They are in Sawpit and Placerville and Ridgway and Norwood. When the construction economy of the east end of the county stops booming, we hope that the tourist economy and economic diversification will maintain the area. The issue is still in doubt. Those that are planning should remember that San Miguel County had a much larger population and a bigger economy in today's dollars in 1894 that it does today.

That boom busted as well.

September 13, 1995

The Keys to the Kingdom and the Secret Plan

It seems that a parking permit is destined to become the key to the Kingdom of Telluride. The kingdom wants to impose by edict what they can't by logic. It goes beyond parking — it goes to a secret plan. We'll get to that later.

The town has a traffic problem and a parking problem. New laws and extensive law enforcement will not solve the problem. You don't believe us? Let us look at some examples.

The town council reduced the speed limit to 15 miles per hour. That is five miles an hour below the engineering and staff recommendations. It means that cars will be on the street longer, increasing traffic. If a car kicks up less dust at that speed, it makes up for it in emissions of partially burned fuel.

Reducing the number of spaces in town by parking strangely designed benches where cars used to be has increased street traffic. Much of the traffic on the town streets is now cars looking for parking spaces. What about the secret plan? We'll get to that.

Regulations should be the last step not the first. There was a comprehensive plan for parking and traffic done by consultants for Telluride in 1990. It only cost $10,000, and with $200,000 management plans on the horizon, we suppose it wasn't taken seriously. The consultants said that intercept parking works best when it is the most convenient way to do business. Regulations and enforcement should only be looked at if no amount of convenience can make the system work.

The town doesn't have the parking lot yet, the gondola isn't running yet, the bus system is on again and off again, but the regulations are being promulgated as a first step, not a last step. If you want intercept parking, why don't you build the lot, implement the transportation plan, and then see if anyone parks there, before implementing a whole level of regulation, regulators and enforcers first.

Is this wonderland, and is the Queen of Hearts in charge?

Speaking of buses, CFeet has dismissed them out of hand. They ran a bus to Placerville for a few months and weren't satisfied with the ridership. There is a single bus a day to Norwood that doesn't run at the times most people commute to work and they aren't satisfied with the ridership. Buses don't run during off-season, so you can't sell your second car if you commute. Buses work to reduce traffic if they are frequent, consistent and they run year round. That has never been tried here. And then there is the secret plan.

Listening to CFeet and the Town Council, they keep calming their outraged constituents by coming up with more permits. Three adults in a car get one, anyone who sleeps on a couch in Telluride gets one. By the time they are done there will be more permits than spaces anyway. It will come to the point that permit holders will be fighting over parking places. That will mean that Town Council and Town Staff will not be able to find a parking space.

The Secret Plan. This year the town lease-purchased for well over a million dollars the Power Company storage yard across from Village Market. Since it wasn't an outright sale, it didn't go to the voters for funding, so statements guaranteeing it would go for parking wouldn't have to be made. The 1990 plan called for a relatively simple, 75-car parking structure to offset spaces being lost through development and regulation in the business district. CFeet and the council have been strangely silent as to the use of this million-dollar purchase. In all of their proposals there has been no schedule for this facility being brought on line. And no further discussion on its use.

Why?

With all the new regulation, the town staff is exploding. Between staff and boards and commissions and elected officials, about 20 percent of the population is involved in governing the other 80 percent, a ratio worthy of Albania. To paraphrase, "Never have so few been governed by so many."

Where will they work, but more important, where will they park? We believe there is a secret plan in the labyrinth of Rebecca Hall to construct a new town hall on the old Power Company lot. It will have an underground parking lot.

Who will get permits to park there? We wonder.

September 27, 1995

⭤

It is Knowledge that Makes Us Free

We attended graduation at the Norwood High School a week ago. Our headline was "Norwood Graduates Ten." More than half of those graduates received scholarships. We don't know if that is any kind of a record, but it should be. What with the fine performance of the senior class and our Knowledge Bowl Team going to the Nationals, Norwood is developing a reputation as a center of learning. We received several calls from people who had read the national press on the Knowledge Bowl Team and wanted to know about moving to Norwood. One lady from Colorado Springs said, "Norwood must a perfect place. A small town with a great public school." We already knew that, but we weren't spreading it around. Besides, the school alone is not the answer. Yes, we have many fine teachers and an exceptional knowledge coach in Jeannie Yamnitz, but in Norwood, education is a community effort. Nationally, membership in parent-teacher organizations has dropped by 50 percent since 1970. You wouldn't know it here. Whether it's a school concert or a science fair or an awards program, or a School Board meeting, the whole town is there. The parents of the graduates deserve much of the credit for Norwood's team effort at education. If learning is not of paramount importance at home, much of what happens at school will be wasted. The area's strong 4-H program adds immeasurably to the educational experience.

How important is quality education to our young people? Much has been written about the rich getting richer and the poor poorer in the United States. The general conclusion from such writings is that we need to spend more on social programs. It isn't so. What we need is more education. Despite a quarter century of massive social spending, the gap between wealth and poverty in the United States has widened. The cause is not a lack of social programs, but the widening gap between the incomes of the educated and of the unskilled. Technology and automation have replaced much manual labor. Low-skilled assembly work has moved to Asia and Latin America. College and technical school graduates are paid very well, laborers are not. College graduates in 1976 earned (nearly) 20 percent more than high school graduates. Last year that pay difference was 50 percent. The trend is continuing and we can expect a wider and wider gap between those with technical training and those without.

Lest you think we are uncaring about the poor, the gap may be widening, but the poor are doing better. Recent European studies have shown that although the difference between rich and poor is less in Europe, the poorest Americans enjoy a considerably higher standard of living than the poor in Europe, even in the European social welfare states like Sweden. Rich Thomas of Newsweek described the American economy as "a rising tide that still lifts all ships, even if the yachts get lifted more than the rowboats." Several decades ago I had a friend who was a black South African studying in America. Scenes of Governor Orville Faubus of Arkansas standing in the schoolhouse door backed by armed National Guardsmen defending the school from several small black children were still fresh in my mind. I asked him how he could have chosen the United States for his education under those circumstances. "Didn't you see those pictures?" He replied, "I did, but what struck me most was their parents had driven them to the school in new cars. Education and economic opportunity will make us free."

Back to Norwood. The seemingly daunting task of raising over $10,000 to send the Knowledge Bowl Team to Orlando turned out to be not nearly so daunting. Contributions have poured in from all over Norwood, and the surrounding area, from Nucla to Telluride. They have been exceptionally generous. We have published a list of the contributors elsewhere in the paper and we sincerely thank them and everyone who helped collect funds. Contributions have been received from five states showing that we have more good neighbors than we knew about.

When Robert Weller from the *Associated Press* came down to cover the Knowledge Bowl Team for the national press, he quoted us having said, "The building may have termites and the roof may leak, but we have fine teachers and fine students and you can get a great public school education in Norwood." We did say it and we are proud of it, but we didn't mean to imply that the great education is because of the termites and the leaks. The lower grades in the school are much larger than the graduating class of ten. The end of the water tap moratorium on Wright's Mesa and the unrelenting growth in the eastern end of San Miguel County will continue the upward trend. The school not only needs repair, it needs expansion. The over-worked gym serves as the home for too many different events. Much needs to be done. The technical center must keep abreast of new technology. Student to teacher ratios cannot be allowed to increase as more students attend the school. The school board, teachers and community members are working on new goals and objectives for the school. One of them needs to be an improved and expanded facility. It will take a bond issue and the taxes to pay off the bonds. It will come before the public for a vote. We already know how we are going to vote. It is the best investment we can make. And our children deserve it.

May 31, 1995

⋯⇒◉⇐⋯

Hollow Victories

A decade or more ago the pent up frustrations of the inner city ghettos exploded in the long hot summers of burning and riots in Los Angeles and Detroit. Faced with the inability to understand how to change their lot and their perception of an untouchable and unchanging other world of wealth and comfort, the ghettos were burned by their own residents. They attacked the only thing that they felt they had the power to change. When it was over their plight was so much the worse.

We are far from the ghettos. But there are frustrations here, and they are deeply felt.

As the State of Colorado moves towards spending a quarter billion tax dollars on a new stadium for the Broncos without asking us to vote, as the Congress and the President posture on spending reductions in an election year, as tax burdens and economic conditions weaken the security of families that have worked for generations to pass their homes and land on to their children, the frustrations increase. We seem to have little direct ability to change the situation. Every candidate promises much, but little changes.

There are some taxes that we have absolute control over. They are the mill levies for our emergency services, our library and our school. We get to vote directly in small elections where every vote counts. We have power over the mill levies. It allows us to take out our frustrations on the things that are closest to us.

We don't believe for a moment that the mill levy lost because the people who voted against it didn't care about or appreciate our volunteers. We do believe, however, that the no votes were aimed at the wrong target and were very shortsighted.

The mill levy for the Norwood-Redvale Fire District raised a total of $32,000 last year. It is not much to run a department. If your home had an assessed valuation of $100,000, you paid about 34 dollars for fire protection last year. It was a lot less than cable-vision or medical insurance or a subscription to *Time* magazine or dinner out with the family. If the mill levy had passed, you would have paid an additional 25 dollars a year. It would have fixed the fire truck in Redvale and would have bought our neighbors who fight fires the protective gear that they both need and deserve. If our insurance ratings are downgraded because of our inability to supply our emergency services with the proper gear, the increase in insurance costs will far exceed our mill levies.

It isn't the only problem. We can take the same tax and government frustrations out on our school and our library. The school building in Norwood has major problems. They will not be fixed without money. That money will have come from a bond issue and a mill levy. We have the same ability to express our frustrations with the state of the state and the country in voting on those issues.

Right here in our own home, we can endanger our fire-fighters, short change our children and starve our library, all in the name of our frustration with Denver and Washington.

It would be very wrong.

May 15, 1996

-◦-═◦═-◦-

Don't Convert Your Dollars to Yen, Yet

A couple of weeks ago, I received a call from the corporate offices of Fuji in New York. An assistant producer for Fuji's Japanese television network was on the line. Her accent was a product of school in Manhattan, not Yokahama.

"We're doing a story on the information super-highway for our viewers in Japan. We would like to find a small western town in a remote area, where the Internet is in use. You know how our viewers like cowboys. We understand you are on the Internet in *North Wood*."

I grew up in New York. I know how to speak to these people. Show any sign of weakness and they go for the throat. "That's *Norwood* lady, and I use the Internet. What's it to ya?"

Now that we were on equal footing she got down to business. "Okay, *Nortwood*. We would like to have a film crew come out with a Japanese director, cameramen and staff, and an American interviewer. We want to do a segment on you in our documentary. Does anyone else us the Internet in *Nortwood*?"

This was beginning to appeal to the performer in me. Even Roudy has never been on Japanese Network Television. "That's *Norwood*, Miss." It never hurts to be polite. "Steve Aagard is on the Internet at the Extension Office, and so is Barbara Youngblood at the library." Barbara is actually on the Marmot system, not technically part of the Internet, but it gives her instant access to libraries everywhere and I didn't think they'd know the difference. She said that was great and the TV crew would fly in Wednesday night and be in Norwood Thursday morning. She told me they would fly into Telluride and stay at the Peaks. We set a meeting Thursday at noon for lunch at Karen's and I rushed off to tell Karen, Steve and Barbara.

Barbara straightened up the library, Steve rushed back from a prairie dog control meeting in Naturita, and I shaved. Karen told me Thursday that she dreamed forty Orientals showed up at the restaurant wanting coffee and the coffee pot was broken. I told her they probably drank tea.

At 11 o'clock Thursday, an hour before they were scheduled to be at Karen's, the same assistant producer called from New York.

"I'm sorry about this, but the shoot is cancelled. After staying at the Peaks last night, the producer decided that Telluride was the typical western cowboy town that they wanted to film. They won't be coming to Norwood."

June 1, 1994

The Lure of the City

Hitler, Stalin and Walter O'Malley, the three most hated men in Brooklyn. The first two for obvious reasons, the third for moving the Dodgers to L.A. I thought about the apartments that now stand over the rubble that was Ebbet's Field. New York had changed.

I returned to the place of my birth for a high school reunion. As the decades pass, I find reunions traumatic experiences. Is everyone more successful, have they gained as much weight, will I remember them, will they remember me? But more of that later.

It wasn't just Ebbet's Field that was gone. The Supreme Court was busily taking a bite out of the Big Apple by deciding that the Statue of Liberty was in New Jersey. And where were the Mets and the Jets? What had happened to my greatest of cities? The ancient walls of Madison Square Garden, where I had seen my first Ringling Brothers Circus and had watched the dazzling Sugar Ray Robinson fight, had been replaced. The great musicians had moved from the elegance of Carnegie Hall and the old Metropolitan Opera to the sterile marble walls of Lincoln Center. K-Mart had opened on 34th Street, just a block from Macy's.

What had New York gained amidst these losses? In the old days, the city had incinerated its garbage on the shore surrounding Manhattan. The EPA put an end to that practice some years ago and the garbage is now hauled in barges to Staten Island, one of the city's five boroughs. The largest structure ever made by man, if you don't count the Tower of Babel, is the Great Wall of China. The second largest is New York's Freshkills Landfill. It can be seen from outer space and it will be full by 2002. Day and night a steady stream of barges hauls the city's refuse to the fill. Not much of a trade for the Statue of Liberty.

Years in the Mountain West leave one unable to afford the $350 hotel rooms of the city and I stayed in a guest room at the Episcopal Seminary on Tenth Avenue. My eldest daughter is studying there for her master's degree and they were kind enough to take me in. After attending her Old Testament class, I left her to her studies and tried to recapture the magic of the city I loved, now so strangely alien.

Manhattan is a walking around town. The people who live and work there have little need for cars. Fleets of buses, ferry boats, and subways move you everywhere and there is so much within walking distance of each neighborhood, cars are generally saved for weekend excursions to the hinterlands.

I took the subway to Columbus Circle. I had ridden the underground trains to my first days of elementary school. I walked along Central Park past the horse-drawn hansom cabs. Central Park was the first great public park in the New World. Built in 1858, its designer said he would create a "wonderland of walks, rambles, lakes, gardens and meadows. Designed not for sport, political demonstrations, concerts or the Metropolitan Museum, but for the contemplative walker. To make life in the city healthier and happier." He succeeded.

I reached the Metropolitan Museum and walked among the Rembrandts and the tombs of Egyptian kings and remembered some of the joys of the city. I went to the Algonquin Hotel and had coffee at the table where Dorothy Parker and Robert Benchly held court in the twenties. I walked between the great lions that stand guarding the steps of New York's greatest of public libraries.

On every block there were green grocers with tempting outdoor displays of fruits and vegetables. The Italian immigrant families that had run them in years past had been replaced by Koreans, but little else had changed. There was more laughter on the streets than anger and contrary to legend, the cab drivers didn't try to run me over.

I took a bus to the East River and looked at the Brooklyn Bridge. An immigrant, John Augustus Roebling, built a suspension bridge of unprecedented length, thanks to the wire rope he invented. He had tied his ropes of wire across one another in great squares to make a bridge infinitely more beautiful than the others that would follow. There were no cars and buses when the bridge opened in 1883. The public worried that the weight of walkers and horse-drawn wagons would cause the structure to collapse. Never missing an opportunity for publicity, P. T. Barnum walked fifteen elephants across the bridge on opening day. The bridge still stands a century later.

I went to the White Horse Tavern and sat on the barstool where the great Irish Poet Dylan Thomas had sipped his last whiskey. I drank to his memory. I picked up my daughter and we had giant pastrami sandwiches and cream sodas at the Second Avenue Deli. We caught a movie — there were 700 theaters to choose from — and then went back to the seminary. Wright's Mesa seemed very far away.

On my last night in the city, I tightened my belt and hoped I still remembered how to tie a necktie and went to the reunion dinner. It was held in one of the city's oldest clubs. Dark wood walls, overstuffed leather chairs, crystal glasses and solicitous waiters greeted my arrival. Of the seventy or so men in my class, about half were there. There were presidents of major corporations, doctors, scientists, lawyers, producers, directors and me. I spent some time looking at my shoes and hoped to remain largely unnoticed.

The president of Hearst Publications came over. "You've been living in a small town in the mountains of Colorado. How did you manage that? I am really envious." He was joined by a television producer and a famous trial attorney. They echoed his sentiments.

Gaining in confidence I replied, "You have to decide what's important. You have to give up a few things."

"Like what?"

"Like being able to stay in hotels in New York."

As I write there is snow falling on the mesa. A flight of geese has noisily landed on the pond across the road and a bald eagle watches them from my tree. There's a fire in the wood stove and the sky stretches to the horizon.

The lure of the city never fades for me, but you have to give up a few things to live here and they are very small for all that is gained.

December 4, 1996

Mayor Peter Spencer (right) and Roudy Roudebush officiate at the Grand Opening of the Doral Hotel and Spa, Spring 1992.
Photograph courtesy of the Scott Spencer family

CHAPTER TWO

On Journalism . . . the First Draft of History

Preliminaries . . .

Longtime journalist and writer Peter Spencer supplied the "Quote of the Day" for the *Telluride Daily Planet* in February 1993. Spencer's quote: Never ask a barber if you need a haircut.

That quote could well serve as Spencer's call-to-arms regarding journalism. As a journalist and editor myself, I covered Spencer when he was Telluride's mayor. I was constantly amazed at his ability to almost immediately cut through the red tape and verbiage to find out what a report or proposed regulation actually meant to the general public. And, at times, the plethora of legalese failed to support the bottom line of such a report or proposed regulation. Telluride's population was well protected from an eager government in those heady days.

Before Spencer started *The Norwood Post,* we had several conversations over the possibility, the potential and profitability of starting a small weekly newspaper in the ranching community that was, in many ways, the opposite of Telluride. I readily took to the naysayer's role, pointing out Norwood's affinity for not trusting "outsiders" — that unless your grandparents, or even better, your great-grandparents had their chiseled headstones standing in the local cemetery, an outsider you would remain. And, I suggested, the local business community figured if someone wanted something, the locals would just come to the store, not read about the inventory in a paid-for ad. But when I saw the flame and passion in Peter's eyes when he spoke of providing a newspaper to the Norwood community, I knew that practical profitability of such a venture was, at most, a tertiary consideration.

Peter and his small staff did not disappoint when the *Post* finally went to press. With fact and persuasion, Peter faced head-on the serious water concerns of Norwood and its surrounding ranches. Its then-mayor and her cohorts, who were running roughshod over the citizens, soon found themselves in his journalistic bull's-eye. A well-informed electorate turned the mayor out to pasture in the next election.

More and more readers began looking forward to Peter's weekly personal columns and their attendant cautionary tales of over-regulating governments and unintended consequences of well-meaning legislation and regulations. Peter's vast knowledge provided readers with plenty of historical perspectives that backed up his conclusions. Over the years, Peter wrote the equivalent of several novels in his weekly columns. He also found himself on the lecture circuit outside of Norwood — a passion for which burned at least as brightly as his call to journalism.

I well remember that night in the Sheridan Bar in Telluride when Peter enthusiastically introduced me to the Eastern couple who had purchased *The Norwood Post,* giving Peter a well-deserved rest from the constant deadline pressure. But, as the new owners plunged further into the dark chasm of tabloid journalism with all its negative connotations, I noticed a slump in those once-proud shoulders of responsible journalism.

After Peter's untimely death, I found myself temporarily at *The Post*'s helm when the ones who had purchased the newspaper from Peter had sullied *The Post*'s reputation, failed to pay Peter the legal debt owed him and, in a moment of shameful irresponsibility, declared bankruptcy and started another weekly tabloid in Norwood. Finding myself sometimes overwhelmed at the *Post*, I would conjure up the great strength of Peter Spencer's spirit when I, like many others, found myself the target of the other paper's viperous editorials and dangerously slanted news.

But in the end, the snakes were driven from the countryside and Peter Spencer once again conquered over evil. May he rest in peace.

— *Bob Beer*

Looking Eagerly for Typos

When you find a creatively spelled word, remember what Andrew Jackson said, "It's a damned unimaginative man who can think of only one way to spell a word."

May 4, 1995

Spelling Aside, It's the Right Size

Selina was pouring me coffee at Karen's the morning after *The Post* came out. Anxious for reviews, I asked her what she thought. It was a safe bet I'd get a positive response. After all, her husband's picture was on page five fighting the fire and I had spelled his name right.

"It's just the right size," she responded brightly.

"Great! You like the long tabloid format and the more readable type we use?"

"No, that's not what I mean."

"You like the length of the stories and the columns and the big pictures?"

"No, that's not what I'm talking about."

"Well, why is it the right size, Selina?"

"It's just the right size to start a fire. It usually takes two *Daily Planets* or *Forums*, and you always have some of the *Times-Journal* left over, but *The Norwood Post* is just the right size."

I'll try not to let it go to my head.

May 11, 1994

⊹⟫═◉═⟪⊹

We're Doing Better in Spelling, It's the Facts We're having Trouble with. Not to Mention Ending Sentences with Prepositions.

Determined not to spell anyone's name wrong in at least one issue of the paper, I checked and rechecked every one last week. My wife checked every name in the last issue against the phone book, just to make doubly sure. Karen Marsing, who is just about our entire staff, checked all the names again. She grew up here and knows nearly everyone in *Norwood Post* country, and how to spell their names. Ah! Sweet success. Issue Three has been out for five days now and we have not had a single call about misspelling anyone's name. (I will revise the above at press time just in case.)

Last week, I wrote that Governor Romer was going to be the first Governor to land at the Nucla airport. I understand that it is traditional in the newspaper business not to reveal your sources, but I will break that rule, just this one time. I think someone told me in the Post Office. It is the first time this Governor is landing there, but as I was soon to find out, there have been Governors before him.

Jean Hughes stopped by on her way to breakfast Thursday. "John Love and his wife Ann used to fly into Nucla all the time when he was Governor. I would pick them up at the airport and drive them to Telluride. They usually stayed at Jack Hawkins' house. Ann loved to hunt old purple glass and there was plenty of it laying around Telluride."

Oh well, maybe nobody else noticed. Then the phone rang. Sandy Williams introduced herself and said she liked the paper, but did I know that Governor McNichols flew into Nucla in 1958 to dedicate Hopkins Field. No, I didn't know that. By Friday, I thought maybe all this Governors' flight plan flap had died down when Jean called.

"Did I remember to tell you that Governor Love flew into Nucla to dedicate Miramonte Reservoir in the late 1960s?"

The situation is getting out of control. I went across to Frances' bookstore to get a cup of coffee and lick my wounds.

Doris Ruffe was there. Doris has lived in Placerville since forever. "Peter, I really liked the article on the warm springs . . . " I wondered what was next. "But you do know that it was called Lemon Warm Springs, not Guthrie Warm Springs."

Doris went on to tell me that people claimed great curative powers for the water. Some said that people in wheelchairs had regained their ability to walk after soaking in the springs. "Some people would drink the water. My father did and said it kept him healthy." I asked Doris if she drank any. "No, it smelled too bad."

I think this week I'll try some.

May 25, 1994

Would We have a Horse on the Front Page if it was the End of the World and Other Myths of Front Page News

It is not true that *The Norwood Post* always has a picture of a horse on Page One. We missed the first issue. I was still learning to take pictures, and the only decent horse picture I had taken missed the feet and part of the nose. Being a newspaper junkie, I've looked at many other front pages, and considering the alternatives, I'd rather see a horse over morning coffee than a car wreck or O. J.'s arraignment. We did put Smokey Bear on the front page once.

There is an old story that's made the round of newspaper junkies — about some national newspaper's Page One headlines — if they knew that the World was going to end tomorrow. Some of the papers and their headlines were: *New York Times*, "World Ends Tomorrow, details on page 7"; *Wall Street Journal*, "Markets React To End Of World"; *Washington Post*, "World to End, Minorities Affected Most"; *New York Post*, "Triple Murder in Brooklyn."

This story gave me pause to think about what would be on *The Post*'s front page if the World was ending tomorrow, and how some of the other local papers might see the same story. I picture the *Telluride Times-Journal* headline, "Town Council Meets To Discuss the End of the World, Aspen Apocalypse Expert Hired." The *Daily Planet* might run "Associated Press Reports End of the World." The *Montrose Daily Press* would probably report "School Board Meeting Cancelled." Just kidding, guys and gals.

What would *The Norwood Post* front page look like on the day before the end of the World? I think the headline could read, "Rodeo Postponed Indefinitely, Moving to Higher Ground." I know that the burning question on everyone's mind is would we have a horse picture. I'm not sure, but I do have this really great shot of the Four Horsemen of the Apocalypse . . .

June 22, 1994

◂═◉═▸

There is a Bright Side to Housing Shortages and We Just Found It.

My friend Robert Weller from the *Associated Press* was visiting in Norwood this weekend. There are quite a few AP people in Colorado, but they are all on the Front Range and Robert covers all of the Western Slope and some of Utah. Saturday night we went to the Cone and swapped tales of tough assignments and exotic locales as newsmen are prone to do. In 20 years of reporting, he had covered everything from wars and revolutions to coronations and abdications in every corner of the globe. I gave him the full benefit of my nine weeks of covering swine weighins and taking pictures of horses. He was really impressed that I had personally interviewed Smokey Bear. I had actually only talked to Smokey's interpreter, not speaking fluent bear myself, but it was Saturday night at the Cone and exaggeration is generally expected.

He was here writing another story, but I knew he was itching for real action. I told him I would take him to an event he had never seen in all his years in the trade. Sunday I took him to the Prairie Dog Shoot in Nucla. It was hot and we got lost trying to find the field where they were shooting, but Robert was on the scent and soon we had some pictures and a few good quotes. We had traveled in separate cars because he was going on to Gateway, and we said goodbye in Nucla.

I got back to my office and five minutes later, Robert showed up. "I couldn't find a place cool enough to write the story," he said, putting his laptop on my roll top. Fifteen minutes later, he plugged his laptop into my phone line and on Monday morning it appeared in both the *Denver Post* and the *Rocky Mountain News*, not to mention papers in all parts of the World. I'll bet he doesn't have a problem thinking of catchy headlines late at night.

But getting to the bright side of housing shortages, Robert had gotten into the fledgling Branch Dividian Compound last week and his story appeared all over the World. Four Dividians had set up shop in a rented log cabin, covered the windows, bought night vision equipment, semiautomatic weapons and had ordered 3,000 more rounds of ammunition. They told Robert that they were focusing on politics and religion and were not confrontational. They only played David Koresh's tapes for "inspiration." Robert had a picture of the cabin and said in the caption that the landlord had ordered them out by July 4.

The day after the story was run, he received five calls asking the landlord's name from people trying to find housing in the Gunnison area. I guess we don't have to worry about them coming to Norwood — there isn't anything to rent. They couldn't afford anything in Telluride, and there's no overnight parking in the RV lot.

June 29, 1994

◦⟶══◦◯═══⟵◦

Okay, We Put a Pig on the Cover. At Least He Had a Home.

We did not cover a single government meeting in this issue. You can blame this on our aversion to government meetings, but it goes deeper than that. Media covers every word, every hiccup, every crackpot political scheme that comes along. If all you read about and all you see on the tube are the endless discussions of politicians, and the endless strident complaints of political wanna-bees, you get the idea that the only thing that happens comes from the government. Most of what is important happens outside the halls of officialdom. Besides, reporting meetings that discuss things but don't decide anything is taking minutes, not news. If they make a decision that changes our lives, it's news. Otherwise leave them alone to make speeches. And let them leave the rest of us alone to go about the business of living.

Put things in perspective. Fair time in *Post* Country is great fun; it's educational and families work together to make it happen. Participation in 4-H, the fair, the community, and our children's lives is the important work of every one of us.

That pig on page one knows that, but he has never had political ambitions.

July 20, 1994

⊶⊷⊸⊷⊶

Murphy's Law is Alive and Well and Living in Cortez

Last Tuesday night we finished *The Post* at 9:30. That is the earliest that we were ever done. It has been as late as 5 a.m. Wednesday morning and as early as 11:30 p.m. on Tuesday, but this was clearly a new record. We went home quite proud of ourselves and somewhat complacent. Then, Wednesday morning at 10:30, I got the call from Karen. "Peter, we've got a problem."

Karen Marsing drives the paper down to Cortez to be printed at 6 a.m. Wednesday mornings and gets back to Norwood at around 2 in the afternoon. Why do we print in Cortez? Newspapers are printed on web presses. These monsters are 50 to 100 feet long. You put several one-ton rolls of paper on one end and newspapers come out the other. The machine prints, does a Chinese paper-folding trick to get the pages in the right places, cuts everything apart, folds the papers and stacks them in bundles. It takes about 30 minutes to print 2,000 papers of 16 pages each — that's 32,000 pages at about 1,000 pages a minute. Sure beats that old mimeograph that we used for our high school newspaper. There are only four of these machines on the Western Slope and only the one in Cortez runs a paper web wide enough to print our large tabloid format. Besides, the press in Cortez has been at it for 104 years and they have figured out the business by now. They print about 20 papers in Southwestern Colorado and nearby Utah. About 4 a.m. Wednesday the control panel shorted out on the press. Larry Housen, the production manager at Cortez, may not have been there all 104 years, but he's been there a long time and knows as much about newspaper production as anyone in the country. If anyone has ink in his veins, it's Larry. Fortunately they use soy ink, so it isn't toxic.

Well, Larry was ready for Murphy's Law, and had spare parts for every relay, resistor and switch in the control panel. From 4 to 6 a.m. they rebuilt the panel. They checked everything out and fired the control panel and were ready to play a couple hours of catch up. They hadn't printed Moab yet and we were next, followed by Dolores and then Dove Creek. Wednesday wasn't the big day anyway. Thursday, when they printed their own Cortez paper and the *Times-Journal* and the *Daily Planet* was a much bigger day and they would be caught up by then. But Murphy had a few tricks up his sleeve and when Larry fired up the panel, they realized that the short had fried the motor. The motor needed to be rewound. As minutes turned to hours and the equipment needed to rewind and balance, a motor that size became further and further away (it finally went to Albuquerque), Karen came home and Thursday morning yours truly went to Cortez, being too nervous to stay here. The *Daily Planet* went to Farmington to print; they are a smaller page size and could do it. Besides, there is something about a daily being a day late that is more serious than a weekly being a day late. By this time Larry had located a motor in San Diego and a technician in San Antonio and all were en route. By Friday morning at 10 I had the papers in the truck and was headed over the Dolores-Norwood road home. It is one of the most beautiful drives in the world, but this time I didn't remember much of it.

Larry told me the press had only been down this long one time before. That was 16 years ago, on the day they were trying to print the very first issue of Jim Davidson's *Telluride Journal*. In the early hours of Friday morning as I paced the floor with Linda Funk, publisher of the very fine *Dove Creek Press,* each of us waiting as if for a birth, she told me that she and her husband had bought the paper 11 years ago. I thought I could get some advice. "When do you get a day off in this business?" I asked hopefully.

"This is it," she said ruefully.

September 28, 1994

⊶⥱◉⥭⊷

Some of the News that's Fit to Print

Journalism is the first draft of history. It must be true. It says so at the top of the front page of our paper every week. Lately we aren't so sure.

The newspaper business is part of an addiction. We admit it. We are news junkies. Reading a half dozen papers a day, checking the AP wire and Reuters, watching CNN and ABC and CBC is part of the business and part of the addiction.

While a brutal war raged in Bosnia for all 365 days last year, CNN's lead story was the O. J. trial on 193 of those days. Will future historians remember 1995 as the year of the O. J. trial? We doubt it. It will be a footnote and probably the subject of future movies and novels, but no one will consider it the defining moment of the year. Perhaps it will enjoy a future revival when some twenty-first century Oliver Stone makes a movie that explains what happened.

We didn't much care what happened then and don't now, but our news junkie addiction brought it back to mind this week. There was a blizzard on the east coast, the kind of visual disaster story that the television news loves, and we couldn't find a single story on the 20,000 American troops in Bosnia. Not in any of the local papers we read, not in the Denver papers and not on the television news programs Sunday or Monday.

It isn't that it is old news. Our troops have just started arriving in force. It isn't that there was so much other news. The government going back to work — at least for a few weeks — was widely reported Friday. Even a big blizzard can't take up a whole paper and Elvis' 61st birthday wasn't until Monday. There wasn't any news on our troops in Haiti either.

You might be tempted to ask why.

The answer, we think, is obvious. It is going well.

The media gave extensive coverage to the 200 muddy cold Army engineers trying to build a bridge in northern Bosnia several weeks ago. All the media reported in detail every problem. When the troops succeeded in bridging an icy river at flood stage with a bridge that could carry 70-ton tanks and finished a day early, Bosnia disappeared from the news. The next time you will see a headline about Bosnia on the front page or as the lead story on TV is when an American soldier is killed or when the news perceives some kind of American screw up.

The media prides itself on being factual and confining opinion to editorials. But the choices of what news is covered are a form of editorial opinion.

We had lots of news to report this week and had to leave some of it out. We pride ourselves on trying to minimize negative news, as difficult as that may be. We don't always succeed. We understand the temptation now after finding out that the two biggest selling issues we have had were the ones that had a local drug bust on the cover and another that had a raid on a wild teenage party reported.

What was CNN's lead story today? "Hollywood Deals with Celebrity Stalkers."

We'll try not to go that far.

January 10, 1996

-⟶⟹⟸⟵-

Two Thousand Pages

Over two thousand pages later, *The Post* celebrates its second birthday today with Volume 3, Issue 2. *The Post* started publication on May 4, 1994 with news of the spectacular fire at the sawmill at the top of Norwood Hill. The fire is still smoldering two years later, and *The Post* is still publishing. We reported that the new dispatch was welcomed in Norwood, and in an aside that turned out to be prophetic, we wondered, "will a new jail get the same warm greeting?"

In what is a replay of our first issue, we have a fire on the front page and hope that rains will come soon and we will avoid the dangerous fire season of two years ago. We reported in our first issue that Governor Romer was bringing his staff to *Post* Country for his Home on the Dome program, and we met with the Governor several weeks later as he got an earful from local residents. Most of the letters in the first issue of the paper were pro and con the proposed goals and objectives for the Wright's Mesa Master Plan. They were later defeated and the process is starting all over again.

The Post was fortunate to find local columnists who can enlighten us on everything from history to gardening and horse-shoeing. National columnists Baxter Black and Click and Clack add their unique views to our paper and we are adding features as we add pages to the paper.

The original *Post* was published in Norwood from 1912 to 1938. We wrote in our first editorial that, "These newspapers duly recorded the milestones of daily life, births and deaths, mar-riages, celebrations. Sometimes an ink drawing of the latest fash-ions from the east would amuse, a serialized novel entertain. The latest news of national politics (not more than a few days or weeks after the fact) would be the talk of the café, and a shooting or a report of rustling would bring outrage or excitement. Advice from the vet or local doctor would be carefully studied; recipes and crafts from local homes would be clipped out and saved. The best horse in a race or the best time in a calf roping would always rate the front page, with little or no attention paid to gossip or scandal in distant cities. Feisty editors would rail against some perceived injustice, and opinions were sometimes challenged with fists or even bullets.

"In an age when mobile populations and scattered families are the norm, the cohesiveness of rural communities is as impor-tant as it was a century ago. The original *Norwood Post* was pub-lished continuously from 1912 to 1938. A revival of the traditional rural newspaper can be a centerpiece in maintaining a sense of connection to one's neighbors and the community as a whole. To that end, the revived *Post* will attempt to chronicle, report, educate and entertain."

In 1995 *The Post* expanded its circulation and news coverage. We currently distribute our papers from Slick Rock in the far western end of San Miguel County to Telluride in the east end. We have a newspaper box on the porch of the Bedrock Store in the western end of Montrose County and are everywhere in Nucla and Naturita. We go to Ridgway and Ouray in Ouray County. And have developed a large readership in Montrose. We intend to start an Ouray County edition this summer. We will expand our circulation to Montrose, Cortez, Dolores, Rico and The Mountain Village. Norwood is and will continue to be our home and we will continue to be Norwood's hometown newspaper as we grow.

We wrote when we started the paper, "*The Post* believes that most of what is important happens outside of the halls of government and although we will cover meetings and politics as part of our obligation to inform our readers, we will devote our most enthusiastic coverage to our children, our community and our daily lives." In our first year we were criticized for not covering enough government meetings. Of late, in the heat of political controversy, we feel that we have covered too much government activity. We will endeavor to correct that imbalance this year.

In 1926, the following was reported in the original *Norwood Post:*

"M. O. Ballard took over the publication of the *Norwood Post* on February 1, but declined to make any rash promises as to what he would do thereafter. He merely stated that he would work for the best interests of the community and had long ago given up the idea that a breathless world waited the stroke of his pen to determine whether it could go on for another seven days, which indicates rare judgment and discretion.

"One very poor man can promise more than a score of good ones can fulfill and while our hopes have a certain bearing on the scope of our accomplishments, it's what is done, not what is intended that counts."

We trust that *The Post* has not disappointed Mr. Ballard.

May 1, 1996

Volume 1, No. 1. The Front Page of the first edition of the new Norwood Post, *May 4, 1994.*

Newspaper courtesy of Leslie Sherlock

CHAPTER THREE

A Few Modest Proposals for Reform . . . or Jousting at Bureaucratic Windmills

⌐Preliminaries . . .

Peter loved statistics. He often used numbers to grab your attention, make a point or win an argument, but mostly for the pure enjoyment that their telling might illustrate either how poorly the government was run or how well we were all doing. Seemed like off the top of his head he could come up with the GNP for 1945 or the population of Passaic, New Jersey, in 1960. One personal stat: Peter was 5 foot 9 inches tall, reached only in cowboy boots, which he wore all the time. Well-worn jeans and denim shirts helped disguise the fact that he was born and raised in Manhattan. Well, at least until he opened his mouth, which was all the time. Peter was a combination of cute and handsome. His broad shoulders and tiny little butt lent to his appearance a bear-like quality — one that provided for some amusement one day while we were shopping. Approaching the checkout, Peter looked at me and said that we wore the same size jeans, 36x30. "We have pant size in common," he said, catching the look of bewilderment on my face. "Mine are 36x30; yours are 30x36." While we never switched jeans, we did share many things, like our recurring resolutions to quit smoking and drinking.

Peter loved politics. He overwhelmed the opponents in the race for Telluride Town Council in 1989, receiving the most votes of any candidate. As mayor from 1990-93, his accomplishments were too many to list. Had he not moved to Norwood in 1993, he might have held office for as long as he wished. With *The Norwood Post,* Peter continued his "fearless leadership" in print, never afraid to shake up the system, uncover government funding waste, or tell it like it was. He did not hesitate to get up in front of hundreds of people at town meetings to voice his opinions, joke with the audience or say what exactly should be done. His ability to laugh at both the target of his scrutiny as well as himself kept us honest and smiling.

Today, we notice that vacant seat at public meetings or the empty bar stool at the several taverns where he regularly held court. We miss how Peter could fill a room with his words, laced as they were with historical perspective and delivered with eloquence and conviction and made larger than life with his booming voice. Gone are his new ideas and relevant gossip. Gone, too, are his optimism and his priceless encouragement to anyone with a good or even developing idea.

For me, Peter's editorial, "Why do They Call it a Party if Nobody is Having Fun?" (March 8, 1995), says a great deal about the man. He woke up in the morning with an enthusiasm for life that most of us have not experienced. He could also "rage" — however briefly — at the ignorance around us, only to recover and devise solutions to the world's many problems. He took responsibility for the brightness of his day and ours. His writing illuminated our lives like a light show with many acts and facts, with rarely an intermission. The ironies of life didn't make him bitter. Human error was to be expected. So was bad news. History not repeating itself was his mission. That Peter could laugh even when things looked most bleak reminds me now that I need to smile more often.

— *Leslie Sherlock*

Women and Politics, and You Really have to be Fearless to Tackle this Subject

Tuesday was Election Day in Colorado. The women voted, too.

The states of the Rocky Mountain West gave women the vote early on. It was the men that voted it in. In Wyoming, women voted in 1869 when it was still a territory. Immediately after gaining statehood, Wyoming was also the first state to grant women the right to vote in 1890. Colorado was not far behind in 1893. The equality of men and women working side by side on the ranches and farms of the west made the women's vote a foregone conclusion. It took the east coast a lot longer. New York finally passed women's suffrage in 1917, nearly half a century after Wyoming. The Nineteenth Amendment was declared constitutional by the Supreme Court in 1922. It had first been introduced in 1878.

On both sides of the issue there were fanciful predictions of the consequences of the women's vote. The *New York Times* wrote after the great women's parade in New York in 1912, "The situation is dangerous. We often hear the remark nowadays that women will get the vote if they try hard enough and persistently, and they will, and play havoc with it for themselves and society, if the men are not firm and wise enough and — it may as well be said — masculine enough to prevent them." Well, so much for the eastern liberal establishment. Grover Cleveland said, "Sensible and responsible women do not want to vote." The predictions on the other side of the issue proved just as farfetched. Mrs. Laidlaw of the Suffrage Party said, "Graft and corruption will end when the women vote; the boss shall be no more." Most of all it was generally believed that, "Best of all, the women's vote would end war — what woman would vote to send her son off to be shot?" They had obviously never met Margaret Thatcher.

Well, what did happen afterwards? People on both sides of the suffrage fight believed that women would vote as a bloc. There would be Democrats, Republicans, and women. We all know it didn't work out that way. *Norwood Post* Country is filled with women-elected officials. Our mayors include Mary Helen in Nucla and Cookie in Naturita. There's June right here in Norwood and Elaine in Telluride. Not to mention San Miguel County has the only county commission in Colorado with a majority of women — thank you Leslie and Anna. They say that politics is a dirty job. Well, fortunately we have the benefit of talented women who are willing to do it.

August 10, 1994

⊹⇌◎⇋⊹

Never Talk Politics on Saturday Night, and Why the Whole Subject should be Left in the Smoke-Filled Rooms

There was a dance at the Hitchin' Post on Pioneer Day and my wife put on her best red dancin' boots and invited me out on the town. There was a one-man band and a good crowd and everyone was in the Pioneer Day spirit. I got involved in a conversation with some friends who make their living ranching. We couldn't talk about baseball — they're still on strike. It was too depressing to talk about the Broncos, and hunting season hadn't started yet, so politics seemed the next logical subject. They had some words of agreement for Baxter Black's column that week on Bruce Babbitt. We talked some about the current situation in Washington and there were few kind words for the job that the administration is doing. I agreed that it seemed to me the President was indecisive on many issues and was depending on the immature ideologues that surrounded him to carry out his programs.

"I don't understand what happened. I had a lot of confidence," I said staunchly. The one-man band picked just that moment to take a break. "I voted for Bill Clinton," I said in a voice much too loud for the momentarily quiet hall.

Now, I consider myself a brave man. This column is, after all, called *Fearless Leader*. I must admit that the looks on my friends' faces gave me pause.

"I don't believe I would have told that," said one of them slowly.

This might be a time to beat a hasty retreat to the men's room, or perhaps buy a round at the bar, but knowing when to keep quiet is not one of the virtues of fearlessness. I was never going to apologize for how I voted in the last election, no matter how badly it might work.

"Wait a minute, how come all you guys are Republicans? That is the party of the rich, the stockbrokers, the savings and loan executives. The Democrats are the party of the working man, the farmer, the rancher, the truck driver," I was warming to the subject. "Don't tell me I should have voted for Bush. He was in the pocket of the extreme right wing. He kept Dan Quayle a heartbeat away from the presidency just to keep the right happy. Besides, in the name of the war on drugs or the war on crime, they are eroding our constitutional rights, seizing property without due process and breaking down doors with no-knock warrants. The Democrats worry about education and health care. The Republicans worry about the banks and the stock markets."

"Well," said my friend, "you are living in the past. The Democrats aren't the party of the middle class. They are the party of the nonworking class. They don't worry about the farmer and the truck driver and the workingman. They worry about the winos who call themselves homeless and the people who feed at the public trough. They don't worry about real education. They worry about everyone feeling good about education. And as for eroding the constitution, when the Democrats take away all of our guns, wait and see what happens to what's left of the constitution."

This was the kind of discussion that could lead to broken bottles and bar stools and we hadn't gotten to any questions that really start the blood boiling like prayer in school or grazing policy. I decided that discretion is still the better part of fearlessness and bought another round.

All of this discussion, however, stayed with me the next day. What has happened to the political parties? Why have the extremes of nearly [every] issue staked out so much ground in each of the mainstream parties? What happened to compromise and to both parties keeping the extreme wings of their constituencies in check and out of their platforms?

The truth came slowly. It is the new public participation in the running of the national parties and the picking of candidates that has polarized politics in this country and paralyzed the congress and made everyone hate Washington. Before the primary system and election-reform, the national conventions were run by the ward bosses and professional politicians. They picked candidates and platforms that they felt would attract a majority of the public. A majority of the public is not extreme, so the parties picked candidates and platforms that were not extreme and could compromise and that could get elected. National election reform changed all that. Now a system of primaries that could only be won with a lot of sound bites on television, costing a lot of money, which needed to be donated by people advocating their own peculiar position, is half the process. The other half is caucuses and party meetings that are only attended by the far right or far left or the far out, all of whom insist on their own one issue being included in the party platform. The great center of the American public is too busy making a living and raising their children and living their lives to participate in this process until things get screwed up beyond our ability to fix them. Maybe we need to get the one-issue-meddlers out of the system and bring back the smoke-filled rooms.

Last week Bob Dole publicly took an oath that he would support term limits. This is an interesting oath coming from a man who has been in office since before most of his constituents were born. An oath for term limits isn't a solution. You can always limit a term by voting someone out and term limits won't let you keep the occasional statesman that comes along. If we go back to the old system and let the politicians run politics, we should require only one oath. Just like the doctors, the politicians should be required to pledge that first "they will do no harm."

October 5, 1994

⊷⫣⊙⫢⊶

If You Don't Know Anything, Please Don't Register to Vote

We are always getting press releases and public service announcements to put in the paper. Some are ads thinly disguised as news (a study by the Aluminum Siding Manufacturers' Association conclusively proves that the divorce rate is lower for families living in aluminum), some are kind of useless (don't forget that it is national calico cat week), some are interesting and useful and we print them (registration for 4-H dog club is Thursday). This week we have been deluged with press releases by various organizations promoting voter registration. The deadline for registration to vote in the

November election is Friday, so if you are not registered and wish to be, now is the time. Many of the releases we received quoted statistics about the low voter registration percentage nationally and the low voter turn out in many elections. They made you feel positively guilty for not voting; it is portrayed as a sin ranking right up there with having too much fat in your diet.

Now on the page facing, we have printed a small reminder about the registration deadline Friday. If you want to vote, please register. But if you don't, it's ok, too. Is that un-American? If they still teach Civics 101 and it is the same as when I took it, it probably postulates that for a democracy to function you must have an informed electorate. That means that the electorate must understand the issues and the candidates. There has been a politically correct move afoot of late to simplify and ease voter registration. Make it easier by registering when you get your driver's license. Don't have literacy requirements, don't have English language requirements, don't have residency requirements. Apparently this trend is prompted by fears of unfairness to some ethnic group. The theory is that any test of competence to vote will be unfair to some group who has a higher percentage of the incompetent. That theory is in itself racist, and yet it is proclaimed loudly by the self-appointed defenders of equality. Besides, if people who haven't taken the time to learn anything about the political process and don't have the educational tools to study candidates and issues are encouraged to vote, how does that offset the votes of those who have? It is an issue of survival as well as fairness.

Many advocates of voting rights for anyone bemoan election by sound bite. The candidate with money to buy 30 second TV spots raises doubts about the other candidate, and whoever raises the most doubts wins. A Bruce Benson spot on the tube last night had someone say, "During the time Roy Romer has been governor, there have been 6,000 murders in Colorado. There are only three people on death row." Now what does that mean? Benson's media consultant must think it implies that had Benson been governor, there would have been fewer murders and more people on death row. Unless the governor also sits on the juries and acts as judge in some cases, it is hard to see how he could have put more people on death row. Murder rates nationally seem to be little affected by which party is in the state house. Lest you think I am picking on Republicans, Linda Powers, in radio spots against Scott McInnis, is accusing him of being soft on crime because he didn't vote for the most recent crime bill. Now I find it hard to believe that any candidate is taking political contributions from muggers, and McInnis is probably as hard on crime as anyone. But it is a nice simplistic accusation and can scare even those people who have no idea of the issues and the substantive difference between the candidates.

Then there are the initiatives on the ballot. These are supposed to help the people straighten out the excesses of the elected officials. The full texts of these initiatives were printed in many area papers last week. If you can figure out what most of them said, let us know. We have read them and have gleaned the following information. Amendment 12 proposes that almost all government be done by ballot issue and loosens the rules for gathering signatures so every crackpot scheme can get on the ballot. Amendment 12 would also make the taxpayers pay for any petition that anyone asked for, and the person asking wouldn't even have to live in the community that was forced to pay. Yes, you can have California-style government right here in Colorado.

Amendment 13 legalizes casino gambling in Manitou Springs, even if everyone in Manitou Springs votes against it.

Amendment 11 would force all employers to pay for workmen's compensation treatment anywhere, even at your local voodoo shaman. We will try to figure out what all of the amendments say and what the candidates stand for and will print what we come up with before the election.

We aren't going to vote for any amendments we don't understand fully, and we aren't going to vote for anyone whose platform consists mainly of casting doubt on the opposition. We hope that maybe this is a trend.

October 12, 1994

⊷⟫⊙⟪⊷

Conventional Wisdom, Those Things that Everybody Knows

"You can't win a campaign without negative advertising."

This seems to be accepted wisdom everywhere. It's not true, of course. The oft-quoted proof of the negative campaign maxim is the Willie Horton ad used by the Bush campaign against Michael Dukakis. Horton raped and killed while on work release while Dukakis was Governor and, therefore, Dukakis must be soft on crime and, therefore, he lost the election and lost it badly. It is interesting to note that the Benson ads saying that sexual molestation went up while Romer was Governor were written by the same consultant as the famous Willie Horton ad. You can see how well it worked for Benson. Does anyone seriously believe that Dukakis would have won if the Bush campaign hadn't run that ad or any other negative ad? Dukakis was a poor speaker, so dispassionate that he spoke like he was on Valium most of the time and couldn't ever articulate any of the issues that were important to the voters. The conventional wisdom should be restated. "Negative ads work only if the candidate can't project a strong image and if the voters aren't paying much attention."

"You can't tell the whole truth and get elected."

This time the example quoted is the Walter Mondale debacle against Ronald Reagan. Mondale said he would raise taxes if elected and he was tromped. Of course, Superman couldn't have beaten Reagan in that election. Mondale's remarkable candor didn't help him, but nothing would have helped him anyway. Besides, look what happened to Bush. He took the opposite tack. He said he wouldn't raise taxes, "Read my lips." After he raised them, he got tromped the next time. It seems as if the voters will tromp you if you tell the truth, and after they figure it out will tromp you if you lie. Therefore, if you are going to encourage the wrath of the voters whether you tell the truth or lie, do the right thing and tell the truth. The conventional wisdom should be restated, "If you tell the whole truth and get elected, you might be able to keep the voters on your side."

November 9, 1994

⊷⇒◉⇐⊷

Why Do We Keep Writing about Politics? Maybe because We Didn't Have a Rodeo This Week.

We spent some time at the Sheridan Bar with Paul Talmey last Friday. We still haven't learned our lesson about talking politics in a bar. Paul is a pollster. His organization is among the best in the business and he counts our Governor among his clients. They are always quoting Paul on TV and in the papers. I promised last week that I would write about the election as soon as I figured out what happened. Who better to help me than Paul? The Friday night crowd was more into talking about skiing and sports than the changes in Congress. I figured I would be safe just asking questions and keeping my voice down.

"What happened, Paul?" I asked.

"The simple answer is that in Washington they vastly underestimated the issues of 'guns and gays' in the rest of the country."

"Oh, so the polls were wrong?" I said a little too quickly.

"No, but some people read them wrong," Paul responded, not the least bit defensively.

"How so?" I said, fearing I was one of the many wrong readers of the polls.

"You kept hearing things like 'the Democrats are gaining with women and minorities.' They weren't. What the figures were showing was that they were losing ground with white males. With the voting rights forces creating black districts throughout the south, substantially reducing minority influences in the remaining districts, most Democrats didn't stand a chance."

"That's something, but there has got to be more to it. That doesn't explain the magnitude of the Republican sweep," I asked, wondering if Paul would like to write a guest editorial.

"Sure, there's lots more. The baby boom generation is aging. People become more conservative as they get older and acquire things they would like to conserve."

"Wait a minute. I know lots of old Democrats, me for one," I said, now on the defensive. Paul was kind enough not to point out that I didn't have that much to conserve.

"Many of the traditional Democrats that remembered Roosevelt are dying out. This is a different generation. The old generation remembered the Democrats as the party of the workingman. This generation sees them as the party of the poor and the minorities. The thing about minorities is that they aren't the majority of the voters."

Well, in this day and age, it is as tough to be a Democrat at the Sheridan as it was at the Hitchin' Post. I wrote away to get some information on the Libertarians, but they haven't won any elections lately either.

November 30, 1994

◆→⧓◆

Term Limits. Did You Vote for Them? Will Those You Voted for Vote for Them?

I never believed in term limits. After all, if you don't like an incumbent, you can vote the rascal out, and in the last election, it happened to lots of rascals and some that weren't. More important, if you get an occasional statesman, you certainly don't want some term limit law preventing you from reelecting him.

The Republican members of the House of Representatives made a promise in their Contract With America before the election that if they had a majority in the House, they would pass term limits in the next hundred days. They were led in that pledge by the new Speaker of the House, Newt Gingrich. Given the considerable support shown for term limits by the voters, that pledge may have helped the Republicans in their landslide.

Politicians are in such disrepute these days that the other argument put forth for term limits is that it will keep the professionals out of the field. I don't know of any other serious endeavor where amateurs are generally thought to perform better than professionals. One of the Republican dissenters in the term limit discussion, Rep. Henry Hyde, R-Ill., apparently agrees. He said, "I think America is always going to need statesmen, and you don't get them out of the phone book."

Well, after counting up the votes in the new Congress, we were convinced that neither Representative Hyde nor I would have our way, and term limits would be a sure thing in the new Congress.

A funny thing happened on the way to Washington. It seems that enthusiasm for term limits, limiting the terms of incumbents, is in direct proportion to the number of incumbents in your party. Within two weeks of the election and two months of the Contract With America, the new Republican majority leader for the House, Rep. Dick Armey of Texas, said that support for term limits may wane now that the GOP will control Congress. He said, "If Republicans can straighten out the House, Americans may not be so enthusiastic about limiting the time a person may serve in Congress."

What about Newt Gingrich, the new Speaker and the architect of the term limit promise? Well, you can always count on Newt. He is as strong in his support of term limits as he ever was. Of course, he did say for the first time last week that any term limit legislation would "not be retroactive," thus relieving current members (himself included) of worries about their job security.

In politics, sometimes everything changes, but most times everything stays the same.

December 7, 1994

⤙⟹⟸⤚

Let's Give the Government a Year Off

North Carolina was the first colony to formally propose independence. The North Carolina Provincial Congress instructed its delegates to the Continental Congress to vote for independence on April 12, 1776. North Carolina's State Constitution provided that the state legislature meet every second year. In the early days, they met in late winter and adjourned in time to be home for spring planting. They came back two years later. In 1968, the state government put before the voters a constitutional amendment allowing the legislature to meet every year. After all, argued the government, how can we expect a modern society to function without continuous government legislative action?

"Very well, thank you," answered the voters. The amendment was defeated by a 3 to 1 margin. There was a common sentiment behind the vote, "No one's life or property are safe while the legislature is in session."

We haven't followed North Carolina legislative action in some years, but we hope that they have kept the same attitude. In Colorado this year, 18 new laws take effect on January 1. That is on the low side as far as states go and most of the laws aren't too bad. Among the new Colorado laws is a rewrite of vehicle and traffic laws repealing obsolete language and revising penalties and surcharges for traffic offenses. There is a law making politicians who get free tickets to sporting events report them on financial disclosure statements. There is a law creating a new certificate from the State Division of Wildlife for hikers, backpackers, and nature lovers. The $1 per year certificate will provide funds for search and rescue efforts. It will also provide funds for non-game wildlife. There is a law establishing the Colorado Catastrophic Health Insurance Act, which allows employers who don't offer health insurance to offer catastrophic health insurance coverage to employees.

California, by way of contrast, has 1,400 new laws taking effect on January 1. They never seem to run out of things to regulate. We haven't been able to get a complete list, but they include state laws mandating dress codes for schools, a work place law preventing employers from banning blue jeans and slacks on female employees (apparently they can prevent male employees from wearing jeans), and a law that allows 14 year olds to be tried as adults for crimes. We can only imagine what other laws they dreamed up at the rate of over 4 per day, 7 days per week during 1994. In Colorado we only passed 1 or 2 per month.

Nearly 400,000 people moved out of California last year. A substantial percentage of them moved to Colorado. Not too many people moved here from North Carolina. In the spirit of the pioneer West, Colorado has generally made its newcomers welcome. It would be well for the new residents to remember why they left California and not try to bring with them the idea that there is a legislative solution for every problem. We hope that the new Congress in Washington follows the Colorado and not the California example.

January 4, 1995

-◦≡◎⊂≡◦-

The Save Us from Ourselves Amendments, or Tinkering with the Constitution, Part I

I have never been very good at balancing my budget at home. At the beginning of the month I always seem to run out of money before I run out of bills. I daresay that others have similar problems. Of course you can borrow money to pay the bills, but then you have added to the next month's bills and sooner or later you have three choices: borrow more, earn more, or reduce the bills. Unless the shortfall is a temporary situation, borrowing more is a short-term solution that creates a long-term problem. Earning more is not always an option. I can't figure out how to reset our newspaper boxes to 35 cents, and a quarter is a nice round number to charge for a paper. Reducing the bills always seems possible, but what with school clothes and braces and filling up the gas tank, it is an elusive goal. The only solution that I haven't tried is passing a law, "You will not spend more than you earn."

Not having the ability to pass laws since I left politics, I am not sure how to go about it. I suppose that I could post a big note on the refrigerator. "Balance the budget or else." Being one that makes frequent trips to the refrigerator would keep the message always visible, but the question comes to mind as to what the "or else" might be. If getting the water turned off or bouncing a check at the grocery store isn't enough of an incentive, what would it take? I used to post a note on the refrigerator with my current weight on it. That didn't work either, so I just stopped weighing myself.

Apparently the new United States Congress has figured it out. They just haven't let us in on the secret. A majority of the Republicans in the House of Representatives signed the "Contract With America" (some pundits have dubbed it the "Contract On America"). It has been printed as a little booklet that the new Speaker of the House waves at every opportunity (sort of the way the Chinese used to wave Chairman Mao's little red book). The Republican majority has promised to pass the provisions of the contract in their first 100 days. They have 92 days left. If you haven't read the contract, don't be embarrassed. A recent poll indicates that 60 percent of Americans don't know what the contract is, and 92 percent of Americans haven't read it.

Some of the provisions of the contract are just fine. It provides that Congress would be covered by the same laws that it applies to the rest of the country. Congress would be subject to OSHA laws and the Disabilities Act and wage and hour laws. I can't wait for an OSHA inspector to assess penalties on Congress for violations. Of course, guess who would pay the bill. Changing the House rules is one thing, amending the Constitution is quite another.

The Constitution of 1787, with subsequent amendments, is not a perfect model for the next century, but it has served us remarkably well for 200 years and should be adjusted very slowly and carefully, if at all. The first provision of the contract calls for a balanced budget amendment and grants the President a line item veto.

First, the line item veto. The argument is that when a budget is sent to the President, instead of having to veto the whole thing if it was too large, he could pick items out of the budget to veto while letting the rest of the budget go through. The theory goes that the President would be able to reduce government expenditures by removing the pet projects of Congress. In the carefully crafted balance that the Constitution gave the three branches of the federal government, the founding fathers gave the ability to tax and appropriate funds to the Congress. They felt that since the House was elected every two years by more local constituencies, they would be more sensitive to the wrath of the voters and would be more cautious, a theory that was proven in the last election. They also felt that giving control of spending to the President would give him too much power. Congress hasn't been very frugal, but Presidents are not generally known for their frugality, either. It would give the President the power to not fund programs passed by Congress that he didn't like, even if they were fiscally responsible. I'll stick with the founding fathers.

Now the balanced budget amendment is another story. We probably should call this the "Save us from ourselves, Mr. Chief Justice, Amendment." The amendment that is being proposed would "compel Congress to adopt a budget in which total outlays for any fiscal year could not exceed total receipts." Now there is a note to post on your refrigerator. The question is what is the "or else." And more to the point, who would do the compelling?

Congress hasn't been able to pass a balanced budget in more years than any of us can remember. The current majority has promised to cut taxes for the middle class, increase defense spending and not touch social security benefits. Houdini couldn't balance the budget after that. If the amendment is passed, and well it might be, and the Congress can't balance the budget, what then? It would be inevitable that the Congress would be taken to task in the courts. Now we would have the Supreme Court ordering new taxes and canceling expenditures for a Congress that cannot.

To implement the Amendment after it is passed, Congress would have to create laws to penalize themselves if they didn't follow it. Would they fine themselves? Would they take their free mailing privilege away? Would they order the capitol police to take them away to jail? Would they be required to post the amendment on their refrigerators and feel bad if it didn't work? They haven't let us in on the secret yet. I hope they do before they start tinkering with the Constitution. Maybe I can use it to balance my budget. I hope it works better than my notes on the refrigerator.

January 11, 1995

Reading the Unreadable

There is a new computer in Washington, D.C. In the abbreviated lingo of the Internet, its name is Thomas.house.gov. The "gov" means it is government owned; the "house" means that it is run by the House of Representatives; and the "thomas" is for Thomas Jefferson. If you have a computer and a modem (the gadget that runs data into sound so it can travel over phone lines) you can read everything that is written or spoken at the House of Representatives. Leaders of both parties have waxed poetic about letting the public in on everything that is going on in government and how it will create public participation in the process, a true Jeffersonian Democracy. The White House has its own system, and the Senate, you can be sure, will not be far behind, though we suspect that their system, in true Senatorial fashion, will be both slower and more expensive.

Having some fairly whiz bang equipment for a small town newspaper, we cranked up the system over the weekend (the net is cheaper to access on weekends), and logged on to the thomas computer. We are convinced that Jefferson would not have been impressed. The central files on the system are the Federal Register. The Register is a report of new and proposed regulations. Every time Congress passes a new law, a small army of regulators writes the regulations that will implement the law. Once the regulations are adopted, they have the weight of law, and the agencies charged with enforcing the law use the regulations as their enforcement bible. In 1963 the Federal Register ran 15,000 pages. In 1993 the Federal Register weighed in at 70,000 pages.

The growth of the Federal Register is continuing geometrically. Its growth is fueled by the theory that no one can be trusted to use common sense in evaluating a situation. Everything must be spelled out in advance, as if all situations can be anticipated. In practice, when there are so many complex regulations no one can understand them, their ability to act as a guide is buried under the weight of the words. How can you use a system that no one can understand completely?

Rather than limiting the judgment calls of those charged with enforcing the regulations, the enforcers have unlimited authority from their ability to find a violation of some unknowable regulation in almost any human activity. Dean Bayless Manning of Stanford Law School stated sadly, "Regulation has become so elaborate and technical that it is beyond the understanding of all but a handful of mandarins."

I am on the board of our local rural electric cooperative. I went to a meeting of the safety committee last month. When you work with 65,000 volts, you take safety seriously. Our safety director must have the patience of Job just to read the rules. It took him two trips from the car, with armloads of books, to carry in the government regulations we needed for just that meeting. Several thousand pages of new occupational safety rules were issued last year. We spent the better part of the day discussing how to implement the rules. We were already in compliance with most of them. Then we got to page 16,362, Federal Register, Volume 59, Number 66, April 6, 1994. (They were up to sixteen thousand pages in the first three months of the year.) We don't have room here to quote the footnotes, authority citations and changes and corrections, but it said, in part, "The employer shall ensure that each employee who is exposed to the hazards of flames or electric arcs shall be prohibited by this rule to wear fabrics either alone or in blends that contain acetate, nylon, polyester, or rayon." Not a bad idea, but the 10-page definition of "ensure" in other parts of last year's register says that education and company policy is not sufficient to ensure compliance. Personal verification is necessary to "ensure compliance." Now it isn't easy to find all-cotton underwear, but striking a blow for freedom and the American way, the committee voted not to require the linemen to show us their underwear every morning. We are risking a fine for "improper underwear ensurance." There is general agreement that there is not a company in America that is not in violation of some OSHA regulation. There are 140 detailed regulations relating to stepladders alone.

In his new book, *The Death of Common Sense*, Philip Howard writes, "Our hatred of government is not caused mainly by government's goals, whatever their wisdom, but by government's techniques." What would Jefferson think if he logged on to the House of Representatives computer and saw the tens of thousands of pages of new rules? Jefferson set the course of the nation in quite a few less words. Of course he was using a quill pen, not a word processor. "We hold these Truths to be self-evident, that all Men are created equal, that they are endowed by their Creator with certain unalienable Rights, that among these are Life, Liberty, and the Pursuit of Happiness." I don't know what Jefferson would have said, but I think that one solution to our currant [sic] morass is to remove all of the word processors from Washington and give the regulators quill pens. Get rid of the misnamed congressional computer. When they find a regulator with the penmanship to draft a new regulation, they could mail it to us and we could tack it up on the bulletin board at the Post Office. I think that Jefferson would approve.

February 15, 1995

⋅✦⟫══⊙══⟪✦⋅

Why Do They Call It a Party if Nobody is Having Fun?

My daddy was a Democrat and his daddy before him was a Democrat. Having lived through the Depression and the Second World War, my father's belief in the Democratic Party was unshakable. We called it the "Democratic" Party, not the "Democrat" Party as many Republicans are fond of doing. Politics was a main subject of conversation at our dinner table and it was inevitable that I, too, would be a Democrat. When Kennedy was shot, I cried. When Nixon used the power of the Presidency to try to subvert the electoral process, I became stronger in my faith. The Democrats were the champions of the working people, the defenders of middle class families, the backbone of down home America. The Republicans were the party of the rich, the cartels, the monopolies, Wall Street, and they didn't care about common folk.

Of course, those are generally unfair generalizations. A quarter century ago, the southern conservative wing of the Democrats was far to the right of the liberal Rockefeller wing of the Republicans. The parties were not homogenous, but each had a broad center that was not far from the mainstream of America. Even the extremes of the parties were far from today's extremes. Barry Goldwater represented the right wing of the Republican Party when he ran for President. During the campaign he was accused of being to the right of Genghis Kahn. By today's standards, he would be a liberal Republican, or maybe a semi-conservative Democrat. Both Hubert Humphrey and Adelai Stevenson were considered the most liberal of Democrats, but they would probably be drummed out of the party for their political incorrectness today. What happened?

What happened is that each party, in an age of sound-bite electioneering and perpetual polling, has purged, by accident or design, almost all of their free thinkers. The change from party regulars picking centrist national candidates to endless primaries and parties controlled at the grass roots level, not by the people, but by single-issue special interest groups that have the stamina and zeal to show up at every meeting, has left the conservative wing of the Democrats and the liberal wing of the Republicans decimated. You can't be a Republican unless you are pro-life, anti-unwed mothers, and against the wetlands. Republican Senators are now asking Mark Hatfield to resign from the Senate because he voted his conscience and didn't support the balanced budget amendment. You can't be a Democrat unless you are pro-choice, for welfare, for wetlands at any cost, and want gay rights. These are just a few of the tests that each party has used to remove free thinkers from their midst. The parties don't overlap anymore. The political wrangling that the voters hate so much is inevitable in these new single-minded groups.

Ben Nighthorse Campbell just switched parties. He was a Democrat of the old school. He thought independently and voted independently. He was pro-choice, but against gun control. He was a good voice for the Indians, but he hated affirmative action. He helped block Clinton's mining and grazing plans. He thought that government was not responsible for us, that we were responsible for ourselves, and he rode his motorcycle without a helmet. When he thought the Republican was the better man for the job, he supported Scott McInnis for his own old seat in Congress. Party orthodoxy has a problem with a record like that, and Ben took a lot of flack for it. His response was to switch to the Republican Party.

Some Democrats would like to see Ben resign his seat in the Senate. After all, they reason, we voted for a Democrat, as if party affiliation is more important than character. I don't think that Ben will be any happier as a Republican. I find it hard to believe he could support Phil Graham for President, or that he would change his pro-choice stance. The problem is not solved by changing parties, the problem is that there is no longer a party that reflects the broad center of the American people.

Maybe it is time for a new party. A party that is socially liberal, but fiscally conservative. A party that takes joy in the free spirit of America. A party that rewards hard work, but takes care of the less fortunate, not because it is a "right," but because it is the right thing to do. A party that replaces endless regulations with goals and allows the people to find their best ways to achieving goals. A party that believes in negotiation, not confrontation and litigation. A party that believes in the least amount of government to do the job, but does not let the government abandon those that are most in need. A party that believes the government is not the best arbiter of morality. A party that has room for a broad spectrum of beliefs and no litmus test for admission.

I don't know if a new party will come along anytime soon. I can't imagine what it would be called. But I bet Ben Campbell would be happier there and so would I.

March 8, 1995

⊹⟾⊜⟽⊹

Paper Shredding

We wrote recently about the explosion of federal regulation in the last twenty years. The 70,000 pages added to the Federal Register annually have created an unknowable labyrinth of hoops for the bureaucracy to put us through. Regulatory complexity and the worship of process over progress has created such bizarre circumstances as $950 million out of every billion is being spent by the EPA's Superfund on lawsuits and paper work, and if all goes well, the other $50 million goes towards clean up. The Occupational Safety and Health Administration has 4,000 rules, and every business in America is in violation of at least one. The excesses of regulatory zeal have caused the new Congressional majority to propose a moratorium on new regulation. Small businesses, buried under the weight of paper work and regulators, cry out for relief. We support a major reduction in federal regulation and a return to goal-oriented rules. However, before we burn all the rulebooks, creating a fire that would most certainly break air pollution regulations over a wide area, we should remember a cautionary tale.

The Reagan Administration worried about the burden of regulation on financial institutions. Savings and Loans were having trouble competing for deposits with banks, mutual funds and bonds. They were limited by federal regulations as to the maximum interest that they could offer depositors. Even if they were allowed to pay more interest, they could only invest in home mortgages within their service area. They couldn't earn enough interest to pay higher rates. Of course, this worked out pretty well for people wanting to build a house. They could save up for their down payment in their hometown Savings and Loan, and then when they were ready to buy or build they could get a long-term mortgage at low rates from their neighbors at their local Savings and Loan. The funds being invested in Savings and Loans started to dry up as interest rates began to soar. The government solution was to deregulate. They first removed any limit on interest paid out. They then allowed the Savings and Loans to loan on commercial real estate as well as homes and they could now loan outside their service area. The one thing that they didn't change was the Federal Deposit Insurance. If the Savings and Loan paid more interest than it could afford or if it invested the money badly and went bankrupt, the full faith and credit of the United States government stood behind you getting your money back. That was a big mistake.

Savings and Loans started to play in the big leagues. It was a lot of work loaning $5 million to 50 different families to build

50 homes. You had to go through 50 closings and then collect 50 payments every month for the next 30 years. The S&L couldn't make very much money that way. Of course, they couldn't lose much either, unless all 50 families went bankrupt at the same time. The newly-deregulated S&Ls were suddenly courted by developers with large projects. A $5 million shopping center here, a $5 million condo project there. One loan instead of 50. And the developers were willing to pay fees to get loans. Three points up front on a $5 million loan gave the S&L an additional $150 thousand profit at the start of the loan process with little more work than closing on just one of those 50 houses. Most of those profits went into new branches and new offices and higher paid staffs. None of it went to individual home mortgages. The farmers in a small town in Kansas couldn't get a home mortgage at the Savings and Loan that had held their money for years. It had been loaned to build a $5 million hotel in a ski resort. Looking at profit projections on the shopping centers and condos for repayment, the S&Ls never realized that everyone was building new shopping centers and condos with this new easy money and that there would be so many that few would make a profit. As projects began to fail, the S&Ls became desperate for new funds. Since the interest they paid was unregulated, but the government was still guaranteeing their deposits, all they had to do was raise rates. Investors from all over the world started shopping for the highest rates. They didn't have to look at the S&L's books or ratings. If the S&L was paying the highest interest, they could deposit their money, and if the S&L went under the next day, the taxpayers would make it good. We're not sure of the final figure on the taxpayer bailout of the Savings and Loans; a quarter of a trillion dollars comes to mind.

Has the government learned anything about deregulating carefully? After spending a quarter of a trillion of our money on the S&L debacle, they are now deregulating some phases of the National Banks. Banks will be able to offer stock brokerage services and buy and sell common stock for customers. They will also be able to sell insurance, competing with your local insurance agent. Competition is good, but the stock trading division of a British bank just took an $800 million loss that destroyed the

300-year-old institution. As our banks enter the stock brokerage business, will the Federal Deposit Insurance Corporation have enough money to cover bank failures? If not, your deposits will still be made good, but the taxpayer bailout will make the S&L's quarter trillion look like small change. A quarter trillion buys a lot of school lunches.

March 15, 1995

⊷⟹⟸⊶

The Limits of Government

About twenty years ago there was a deranged talk show host in the movie *Network* who urged his loyal listeners to open their windows and shout at the top of their lungs, "I'm mad [as hell], and I'm not going to take it anymore." They did. At the time, all those people shouting out of their windows seemed a little far-fetched. It doesn't seem so farfetched anymore. The movie never made clear what those shouters were mad about, indeed, they seemed united only in their rage and in their parroting of their hero's sentiments.

There seems to be a lot of shouting out of windows today. The talk show hosts are only a small part of the rage. The message is repeated constantly, write your Congressman or the President, or call your school board member or your planning director. Tell those government types that they are fools and parasites and tell them at the top of your lungs as rudely as possible.

The anger seems to come from one of three beliefs: the government is doing too much, the government is doing too little, whatever the government is doing, it is doing wrong. Sometimes all the beliefs are held simultaneously.

Part of the problem we are having with government is that we are expecting it to do things that no government has ever been expected to do. William Bennett, author of *The Book of Virtues*, tells the story of the second presidential debate in the 1992 campaign. One questioner asked the three candidates, "How can we, as symbolically the children of the future president, expect the three of you to meet our expectations?"

"I would have told that guy to get a hold of himself, get a life," said Bennett. "The government is not your father . . . take care of your own problems. If there's a catastrophe, a national emergency, then the government should step in."

The government does pretty well with national emergencies and catastrophes. Hurricanes, floods, earthquakes, forest fires, threats from foreign invaders — they don't get much better at handling these things than our government. Mad bombers, living in their delusional universe, can always blow something up and cause destruction, but federal law enforcement did a great job tracking and catching the perpetrators of the carnage in Oklahoma City and at the World Trade Center.

Well then, what are we so mad about? We are angry about being overwhelmed by the metastasizing of government regulation into every phase of our lives. Yet every time there is a plane crash, or a car wreck, or a case of cancer, or a case of food poisoning, the public is clamoring for new government rules to make everything totally safe. You can hardly watch a television news feature without seeing people calling for more inspection of something or for the police to baby-sit their children.

We just can't stand the government messing with our economy and interfering with our business and free enterprise. Nevertheless, the minute the economy starts to falter, or prices go down, or unemployment goes up, we want Washington to jump in with a quick fix. Woe be to the politician that has an economic downturn occur near election time, as Bush and countless politicians before him have found out. Of course, the government is controlled by the economy, not the other way around. In the '60s, the government tried Keynesianism. Tweak taxes and spending and keep the economy on an even scale. It didn't work. In the '70s they tried Monetarism. Keep the money supply growing steadily and defeat inflation. It didn't work. In the '80s they tried Supply-Side-ism. Lower taxes and see the increased economic activity eat the deficit. It didn't work either and we are still paying for it. We can hardly wait to see what new theory they will try in the '90s.

The government isn't very good at fixing the economy, but we keep asking them to. They can't fix morality either. They can't legislate away the uncertainties of life. This is America. There is a certain lack of safety that comes with freedom. If we expect the government to make everything totally safe, including our jobs, our health, our comfort, our families, we will have to give up most of our freedom in the process, and in exchange we will get our government trying to do the very things that they aren't very good at. We must look at ourselves, and what we are expecting, before we blame the government for not meeting our expectations.

The biggest complaint that we have about the elected officials is that they aren't listening to us. Of course, that is only fair. We aren't listening to them either. Democracy can only function if the people are informed. No amount of information will help inform anyone if we can't hear it over our own shouting.

May 3, 1995

-+≡◉⊂≡+-

Getting the Government Off Your Back, 1995 Style

Last week, we quoted Hugh Downs in the paper as saying, "Freedom and equality are not liberal or conservative property, they are simply American." That is an upbeat thought and we think it is true. The United States Senate needs to post it in their lounge. Last week, the Senate voted, with broad bi-partisan support, 86-14 in favor of the so-called Exon amendment to the Communications Reform Act. The amendment was titled the "Communications Decency Act."

Neither Senator James Exon nor his co-sponsor Senator Daniel Coats of Indiana have ever logged on to the Internet. They have, however, determined a broad policy for regulating all of cyberspace. The amendment criminalizes all use of indecent language defined as the "seven dirty words" you can't say on broadcast radio and criminalizes all communications deemed "annoying" or having any sexual content. These rules apply to any information on the net that might be available to minors, which is everything. Under the rules, if the Repertory Theater in Telluride posts the script of Shakespeare's *Merry Wives of Windsor* on the Infozone, they can go to jail, and I can go to jail for telling my 4-H computer club how to log on.

Having taught quite a few people how to use the Internet, we determined that it isn't like television or radio where you turn it on and are inundated with pop culture right there in your living room. You really have to work to find the trash that lurks in the distant corners of the net. And the trash isn't any different than what you find in some books or movies or videos. If the Communications Decency Act is playing to parents, fearful that their children will stumble by accident, or design, onto something terrible in cyberspace, it is the wrong way to do it. There are somewhere between three and five million host computers on the world wide net and nearly 50 million people accessing them. All of the law enforcement in the country couldn't police them, and since many of them are out of the country, it seems that even with a lucky find, arrest and prosecution would be most unlikely. If you want to protect your children from access to smut, don't look to Washington for the solution.

There are several solutions available without totally tearing up the Constitution and without putting Barney in charge of electronic communication.

Don't buy your children a computer is the most extreme. It is the equivalent of not teaching them to read to protect them from written smut, but it is probably preferable to having Senator Exon decide what we can access.

Only allow your children to access reliably moderated computer bulletin boards. A moderated bulletin board or discussion group is one where the postings are screened for appropriateness. The kids' section of the Infozone, the Kid-Net and others are among the better ones.

Obtain a computer program like "SurfWatch" which establishes a parental lockout on any Internet locations that offer sexually explicit materials. The Information Highway Parental Empowerment Group, a consortium of computer software companies, is working on new lockout programs.

Do your best to teach your children that there is much constitutionally protected speech that is not in their best interest and they would do well to avoid [it]. Not an easy task, but the best of solutions.

I always thought that it was the conservative Republicans who wanted the government off our back and the liberal Democrats who wanted to regulate us more. I am finding that once they get to Washington, they all want the government on our backs, just for different reasons. The liberals want the government to make us wear motorcycle helmets and seat belts and think Washington will do a better job of setting highway speed limits in the Gunnison Valley than Colorado will. The conservatives think that Washington shouldn't regulate any of those things, but should regulate what we read and what we watch and how we use the language.

Frankly, Americans have always taken these things on themselves, and should continue to take responsibility for their lives. Every time we lobby Washington to fix something, they respond and we come away with more regulation, less responsibility and less freedom. Hopefully the House of Representatives will undo the Senate's folly.

June 28, 1995

-◦⇒◎⇐◦-

A Nation of Immigrants

America has been justly described as a melting pot. The 60 million or so immigrants, who in large measure people this country, became, within a generation, Americans. It wasn't just that their children became citizens by birth. They lost their accents and native dress and old country values within one generation, and by the next didn't understand the Polish or German or Cantonese that their grandparents had spoken. By the third generation, they were no longer Chinese-Americans or Polish-Americans, they were unhyphenated Americans. They had become gum chewing, freedom loving, baseball playing citizens of the U.S. of A. Everyone knew where the earlier generations came from, but they themselves came from America. It makes for a cohesive country that can have a national will and can accomplish wondrous things.

There is a disturbing trend back to hyphens. Perhaps it started in the '70s when the original Civil Rights Act was passed. The Census Bureau was charged with counting all kinds of ethnic groups so that the government could find out by the numbers if there was discrimination. If the population of your state was 7 percent Samoan, but your state university only had 3 percent Samoans, then you must be discriminating against Samoans. If 20 percent of your city was of Mexican descent, but your factory was only 19 percent of Mexican descent, you must be discriminating.

The Census Bureau had a tough enough job just counting everyone without having to figure out where their ancestors had come from or what shade of skin they wore, or how their eyes were shaped. In any event, there were far too many permutations for the Census Bureau to fit on their questionnaires. After all, if you had to count Samoans, how about Fijians and West Indians and Costa Ricans and Puerto Ricans and Mauritanians and Slovaks? Not to mention the Tibetan who lived in Dublin for twenty years and had changed his name to O'Malley before immigrating to Los Angeles. As instances of past discrimination would be redressed to later generations, the bureau had to trace back ancestry. This could be a daunting task. If the parents were a marriage between a Costa Rican and a Puerto Rican, the child would be an entirely new ethnic group, a Costa-Puerto Rican-American. A category only a bureaucrat could love.

The Census Bureau solved this problem with one of the most audacious, though largely unnoticed, acts of the twentieth century. They created their own ethnic groups. It was simpler and cheaper than using the real ones. Never having been too surprised by the intricacies of government logic, we were shocked, however, at how many people have bought into these newly created ethnic groups.

Do you think we are exaggerating? Before the Census Bureau created new, simpler ethnic groups, there used to be, living in New York City, Puerto Ricans and Cubans and Mexicans and Costa Ricans and a few Venezuelans. If you wanted to get into an argument, all you had to do was call a Cuban a Puerto Rican and they would pointedly refute your assertion. There aren't any more of those guys in New York now. They are all Hispanics. The Census Bureau defined this new category in the '70s and now it is one of the fastest growing segments of the population. The Equal Employment Opportunity Commission then started sending out forms asking employers to list by job category how many Hispanics they employed. In case an employer wasn't up on the new ethnic groups, the directions said that they should count as Hispanics any "Spanish surnamed Americans" in their employ. It seems that the E.E.O.C. had further defined Hispanic as being passed along by the father. Now, of course, if Mr. Gonzales married Mrs. Fujimoto, their offspring would be Hispanic if the children took his name. They would not be Hispanic if they took their mother's name. We have no idea what they would be if they followed the hyphenated trend and were Gonzales-Fujimoto. They also created "Pacific Islanders" to take care of the Samoans and Fijians and the like. And they managed to create Asian-Americans to lump the Chinese with the Cambodians and Laotians. An uneasy alliance if ever there was one.

It is of value to know the roots of your ancestors, but to try to take this melting pot and separate it back into different kettles is neither possible nor desirable. It is not possible because the pot keeps on melting and little Gonzales-Fujimoto ends up marrying O'Malley and confuses the Census Bureau even further and doesn't want to be anything but an American. The distinctions are arbitrary and in many cases useless.

We can look at countries that have done a very good job of preserving their differences, some for thousands of years. Bosnia comes to mind. There are Bosnian-Serbs and there are Bosnian-Muslims. Perhaps the Serb's unconscionable destruction of Sarajevo is caused by the fact that Christians and Muslims have lived there peacefully. A trend too shocking for them to contemplate. Then there is Rwanda. The Tutsis and the Hutus have always viewed themselves as Tutsi-Rwandans and Hutu-Rwandans. It has been a strong enough view that the Hutus massacred over half-a-million Tutsis last year for being Tutsis and indications are that the Tutsis would like to return the favor.

The country must provide opportunity for all of its citizens and that can only be accomplished through a strong national will that emphasizes our common beliefs and goals, not our differences. On the Fourth of July, we should remember that the diversity of our population has given America much of its culture, and talent and creativity; but it is the melting pot, the common American heritage, that draws that population together and gives us our strength as a nation.

July 5, 1995

━━◦═◦═◦━━

The Only Certainty is Death and Taxes

Elsewhere in this issue we report on the difficulty of passing on agricultural land. Inheritance tax rates as high as 68 percent on agricultural land have created severe consequences to families trying to pass their family heritage to their children. These rates, passed in 1986, are hastening the dissolution of family agriculture and encouraging the subdivision of agricultural lands and the concentration of corporate farming. Congress, which is anxious to lower capital gains taxes, should give reform of inheritance taxes on agricultural lands a much higher priority.

Some weeks ago, while writing about the difficulty of budget reform, we wrote that in light of the major cuts necessary in some very important programs, perhaps tax cuts should not be a high priority. We haven't changed our mind. But all taxes serve to create policy as well as to raise funds. If we give tax credits for solar energy or for renovating historic buildings or for creating open space, we will have more solar heating systems, we will preserve more historic buildings, and we will preserve more open space. If we put excise taxes on luxury cars and yachts, we will buy fewer luxury cars and yachts. It would seem if we put our highest tax rate on leaving the family farm to our children, then there will be fewer family farms. In Colorado, the state puts up a sign at Centennial Farms. These are farms and ranches that have been operated continuously by the same family for more than a century. When we pass one of the Centennial Farm markers, we marvel at the determination of the generations that worked that land through good times and bad. Without a significant reduction in the inheritance taxes on these properties, we fear we will see fewer and fewer of these farms, until they finally disappear altogether.

"Right on," you say. "Let's cut all the taxes. Staggering taxes are destroying our savings capacity and our competitive position in the world."

"Well, yes and no," we say.

"What," you say. "Don't tell me you are in favor of our impossibly high taxes and big government?"

We certainly would like smaller taxes and smaller government. But we need to figure out where we are before we can figure out where we are going. The Organization for Economic Cooperation and Development in Paris keeps track of tax statistics for the 24 leading industrial countries. In the United States, 29.8 percent of the Gross Domestic Product was taken by taxes. The average for the 24 nations was 38.7 percent, 9 points higher. Only Turkey and Australia were a bit lower at 29.7 and 29.6 percent respectively. The countries that we compete with in world trade were all higher. Japan, Germany, Great Britain, France and Italy all have significantly higher tax rates than the United States.

That is the good news. The bad news is that the average U.S. production worker with three dependents takes home 81 percent of his gross wages. The average for the 24 industrial countries is 85 percent. A flat tax, as has been proposed, would put the average worker at a worse disadvantage. The tax system needs fixing, but it is not the worst by any means.

Before you start calling us a "tax and spend" bleeding heart liberal Democrat — we admitted to being a Democrat in this space before — we think that an overall reduction in government spending would be a good thing. We think that tax inequities need to be fixed. We also think that the spending reductions need to come first. The Republicans have come up with a plan to balance the budget in seven years. The President has come up with a plan to balance the budget in ten years. Both plans are brave efforts. It would be cynical to suggest that since both plans put their largest and most painful cuts into the last two years, after two presidential elections have come and gone, that there was any sign of cowardice in the proponents.

We have written about the difficulties of federal budget cutting. We have a few suggestions. We would suggest scrapping, in their entirety, the Education Department, the Energy Department, the Commerce Department and the Small Business Administration.

Why did we pick on these four departments? This may sound like heresy, but the country did reasonably well without a federal effort at education for its first 200 years. The Education Department promotes outcome-based education. The outcome of the federal effort at mandating educational standards to states and local school districts has not improved college admissions, dropout rates or test scores. Based on the department's own standards, it has flunked out. The Energy Department has done a good job at subsidizing well-connected parts of the energy industry and little else. The Commerce Department has the best-dressed bureaucrats this side of the State Department. They spend most of their time hanging out with textile and steel executives and taking foreign junkets to "promote American products." One good Coca Cola executive brings more business to the United States than the whole Commerce Department. The Small Business Administration has managed to take the risk out of bank loans to small businesses through guarantees. These riskless loans for banks make sure that banks are extremely reluctant to make any other kind of loans to new businesses. The SBA generally evaluates its loans on the borrower's ability to write a great looking business plan and has little knowledge of the local market or the borrowers' abilities.

Have we solved the federal budget problem? Can we now lower taxes? Not exactly. Closing up those four major federal agencies would only go 13 percent of the way to a balanced budget. It doesn't get us there, but it puts us on the way to lower taxes.

July 19, 1995

A Billion Here, a Billion There

After all our writing about balancing the budget and all our requests for help, someone finally came to the rescue. Anna

Houser stopped by on her way to work and left us a study on congressional pensions. It seems that members of Congress contribute 8% of their salaries to pension plans. That covers about 20 percent of the total pension payout. Taxpayers pick up the other 80 percent. House members earn $133,600 a year and with only 20 years' service can begin collecting, at age 50, $72,000 per year for life. It gets adjusted for inflation each year as well.

Anna's diligence inspired us to look for more government largess. We found it at the Pentagon.

Wasteful spending added $29 billion to defense budgets in recent years, arms control and taxpayer advocacy groups say in a report released last week.

In their study, "The Pentagon Follies," the Council for a Livable World and Taxpayers for Common Sense cited such examples as a $10.4 million fitness center planned for the Puget Sound Naval Shipyard in Bremerton, Wash., construction of a third golf course at Andrew's Air Force Base in Maryland, an expensive dairy herd at the U.S. Naval Academy, and a door hinge for the C-17 cargo plane that cost $2,187.

Defense Department spokeswoman Susan Hanson said she had not seen the report, but that allegations of waste are pursued and the problems often are corrected quickly. And some of the cases the report labeled waste can be justified, she said.

"Military personnel are entitled to and do need to have some recreational activities made available to them," Hanson said, referring to sections of the report critical of golf courses and fitness centers.

"We need to look at each one of those incidents," Hanson said. "Such things are certainly reviewed fully in the department."

John Isaacs, director of the Council for a Livable World, credited Defense Secretary William Perry with aggressively seeking efficiency and cost savings throughout the military. The point of the report, he said, was to counter those who attack government waste in domestic programs while advocating more money for defense.

"Those who would simply dump money in the Pentagon budget and say there aren't the problems here as with other agencies, they're looking with blinders," Isaacs said.

The group culled examples of wasteful spending from press accounts and government reports and audits. Among them:

- Congress included $10.4 million in this year's defense budget to construct a second physical fitness center in the Puget Sound Naval Shipyard in Bremerton, Wash., even though there was no apparent overflow in the existing gym.

  "The Naval Shipyard already has a fitness center that includes racquetball courts, tennis courts, volleyball courts, a basketball court, three softball fields, a swimming pool and a gym with Nautilus equipment and free weights," the group said. "What's more, there are 10 private gyms within five miles of the base. During this time of budgetary constraints, $10.4 million for a gym we don't need looks more like fattening pork than the road to good health."

  Puget Sound Naval Shipyard spokesman John Dennis said the report is way off base. He said growth has overwhelmed services available on the base.

  "In the last few years, due to closures of other naval bases resulting from downsizing, the military population at Puget Sound Naval Shipyard has more than doubled," Dennis said. PSNS is now the second-largest Navy home-port on the West Coast, he noted, accommodating 10,000 active-duty sailors and a dependent population of 19,000.

- The Naval Academy in Annapolis, Md., maintains a herd of 319 cows dating back to a bad-milk incident early in the century. Annual cost: $1.2 million. The academy says it is working out a plan to sell the cows.

- Using funds from its Morale, Welfare and Recreation program, the military leases part of a 287-room hotel outside Disney World in Florida. Because of what the report described as bad management, the hotel requires an annual federal subsidy of $27.2 million to break even.

- The third golf course at Andrews Air Force Base will cost $5.1 million. Base officials defend the project, citing increased use at Andrews and other military installations. The report counters that the suburban Washington course is likely to be used by members of Congress and other government VIPs.

- A C-17 door hinge that had to be manufactured hastily by McDonnell Douglas Corp. for $2,187 after a subcontractor failed to provide the part. It should have cost $31.
- Poor financial management practices and record keeping that have resulted in the Pentagon being unable to account for nearly $15 billion in expenditures over the past decade.
- Weapons programs that were canceled despite hefty investment, including $2 billion on an Air Force radar jammer, $4 billion on the TriService Standoff Attack Missile, and $3 billion on the Navy A-12 fighter.

We're still looking for more ways to cut the budget. We need all the help we can get. If you have an idea, let us know. Maybe we should start closer to home. A $200,000 growth management study funded jointly by San Miguel County and the Town of Telluride seems to have run out of steam, if not money. It was awarded to two consultants from Pitkin County, one of whom is gone and there is little to show for the effort. Telluride has been investing in a "Cultural Master Plan," a term we haven't heard since Joseph Stalin died. Sometimes it seems like a hopeless task because every time we think of an idea for reducing government largess, someone comes up with new boon-doggles.

April 3, 1996

⊷⟹〇⟸⊶

Freedom and Security

The tragic loss of life in the PanAm bombing and the pall cast over the Olympics by the pipe bomb in Centennial Park have brought terrorism to the forefront of American thought. Following the tragedy in Oklahoma City and the bombing of the World Trade Center in New York, we have suddenly lost the perceived immunity of our country to acts of terrorism. We have barely noticed the bombs of the last decade in London, Paris and Tel Aviv. They saddened us momentarily, but they seemed local tragedies, oceans away.

The evil lunatics who perpetrated these brutal acts must be hunted down, even to the ends of the earth, and killed. They have no place in the human race. We cannot let terrorists prevail.

However, there is a danger in the reaction to terrorism that may aid terrorists in their cause. If it is the goal of the terrorist to inspire terror, then we must deny them that goal. We cannot let them set our agenda; we cannot let them control our lives through fear.

If we do, then they have won.

There is a greater danger that reaction to terrorism can engender. In the election year, every candidate wants to be shown as the politician of deeds, not words. They want to take action. Some of the proposals are necessary: better airport security, better tracking of baggage. Our airport security systems have been designed to stop the rash of hijackings of the '70s, not the mad bombers of the '90s.

Other proposals have less direct impact on potential terrorism than they have on government expansion.

The government is already requiring the airlines to request photo IDs for boarding passengers. How difficult is it for a bomber to get a fake ID? Computers and desktop laminators have provided fake IDs for everyone from illegal aliens to teenagers trying to buy a beer. Will busses, libraries, government buildings, trains, elevators, rock concerts soon require the same? Will the next bomb cause us to be issued some new form of ID and will the bureaucracy formed to track terrorists' movements be someday tracking everyone's movements? Will we soon be issued travel papers and hear "Your papers please" on every trip?

You may think that is farfetched.

The President's proposals Monday for new legislation to combat terrorism include requests to tap phones and place tracing devices on phones without court orders. Those proposals have been warmly embraced by both parties. Will unlimited government phone taps improve America?

We don't think so.

It was Jefferson who said, "Those who would sacrifice freedom for security neither deserve them nor achieve them."

Those are words to remember or the terrorists will have surely won.

July 31, 1996

Well received by its
readers in the
western counties of
the state, the Post
was also recognized
by the Colorado Press
Association for its
journalistic and
editorial excellence.

Photo courtesy
Deb Jacobs

CHAPTER FOUR

Thoughts from an Oxygen-Deprived Mind . . . or I Just Checked In to See What Condition My Condition Was In

Preliminaries . . .

When I first met Peter Spencer, he and his family were living in an old house on Pacific Avenue, the former residence of a well-known contraband pharmaceutical salesman who was on a Federal vacation at the time. We often wondered what had transpired behind those old walls, and since there were many little secret cubbyholes, we often wondered which secret place held the missing fortune. We never found it, but the wealth that I gained from knowing Peter Spencer was a fortune unto itself.

Peter was one of the first computer gurus in Telluride and somewhat of a mentor to me. We became closer friends when he ran for mayor of Telluride. After many a philosophical discussion of a political nature, usually held at the Sheridan, Elks, or the Last Dollar over cocktails with many of the local pundits, I began to grasp the immense intelligence this man possessed. He could always cut to the chase before most people knew the rabbit was loose. After he succeeded in getting himself elected, I remember when he received his first Town Council Packet at his small office. The damn thing was six inches thick and included a draft of the proposed budget. Peter quickly scanned the pages and about half way through he exclaimed, "There! Right there! That is where they are squandering money."

"Where?" I asked.

"Right there, line 568," he said.

I looked and saw only columns of numbers with obscure sounding titles attached. "What are you talking about," I asked.

"Here! See, back here, on page 126. Now, look at the number on page 291. They don't add up. Jeez, what a mess."

My only reply was, "Let's go to the Sheridan. The town council always squanders money. It's their job."

"Ah, but this is not the same old song and dance," Peter said.

I could neither see nor comprehend what this man had seen and understood so quickly and completely. But something was there and it was not Kosher.

As the years passed and Peter moved from one project to the next, always the restless entrepreneur, we became closer friends and confidants. His ability to deal with any situation in a concise and intelligent manner made him a friend to everyone and an enemy to none. Peter was always fair in negotiations, always honest, and always respected you, win or lose. That is why we, Allen Pattie and myself, put him on the Board of Directors of the Gin Festival along with Lars Lundahl, Peter Langstaff, and Hadley Thompson. Lars could sing and dance around any trouble we got into. Peter Langstaff could act his way out, and Hadley could bail us all out of jail. But we figured only Peter Spencer could get us a pardon.

But it was always his capacity and quest for knowledge that held my amazement. Peter was not as much a student of history as he was an arbiter of it. His vast knowledge of the past would be invoked in the present many a time during his political and journalistic career.

Anyone who has ever conversed with Peter knows that he sometimes seemed to not pay attention to what you were saying. He even went so far — on more than several occasions — to *read* while someone was talking to him. But then, out of nowhere, he jumped right back into the discussion, not losing a beat. He was listening all the time.

Peter's thirst for knowledge was passed on to his children. I remember one Telluride Bluegrass Festival, when Peter was out front with Meghan and I was working backstage.

Riders in the Sky came on stage and they invited the kids to come up for a sing-along. Meghan was the first kid up on stage and she showed no sign of stage fright. Ranger Doug asked her what she wanted to be when she grew up. Without missing a heartbeat, Meghan replied, "I want to be a paleoanthropologist." I think she was 5 years old at the time. Peter just shrugged and said, "Well, that would be alright. Last week she was going to be an astrophysicist." Two of the band members, Ranger Doug and Woody Paul, hold a Master's Degree in Literature and a Ph.D. in Theoretical Plasma Physics, respectively. Ranger Doug was silent.

I shall miss my friend for the rest of my days, and I often think back on the times we had — the conversations, the Gin Festival, the Jefferson Davis Memorial Brunches, the Cheshire grin and the bellowing laughter of the most intelligent man I have ever known.

Randy Sublett

Another Great Headline We Wished We Wrote, and Why Denver Needs to be Moved

I am always looking for examples of great headlines in other papers. Maybe I can learn something from them. This week there was a story in most of the Colorado daily papers about the mosquito problem at Lowry Air Force Base. Wetlands on the Denver air training facility, surrounded by private homes, have turned into a major breeding ground for mosquitoes. The Air Force would like to spray them, and the neighbors have called congress, the mayor, the city council and everyone else whose number they could find. The trouble is that being federal wetlands right there in the middle of the city, the EPA won't let them spray. The Clean Water Act Enforcement Manager for the EPA in Denver suggested putting bats at the site. He said, "Bats can consume tens of thousands of mosquitoes every night." I read that somewhere myself, but he would probably have to wait for 20 years or so for the trees to grow on the barren Lowry to house them, or else plant poles in those wet-lands to hold bat houses. I don't think they let you plant poles in the wetlands, not to mention trees. Besides the trees would probably soak up enough of the water to dry up the wetlands before they were tall enough for the bat houses.

The real solution to this problem is to relocate Denver. They built it in the wrong place to start with. Several weeks ago we suggested that they reintroduce wolves to Cheesman Park in Denver as the first step. Denver was settled very late in the history of the West. In the first half of the 19th century, the tribes that surrounded the area would meet to trade and have a powwow in the spring and the fall at the confluence of the Platte River and Cherry Creek where Confluence Park stands today. By the 1840s traders from the east attended these powwows. In about 1848, they built a permanent trading post. One of the Arapaho chiefs, taking pity on these city folk, advised them the entire area was unsuitable for settlement. When asked why, his response was, "Smoke no rise from Tipi." Besides, there wasn't a tree as far as the eye could see, and there was never enough water to grow one.

The natives were fully aware that the Front Range in general and the Denver area in particular were unsuitable for permanent settlement. The inversions of 150 years ago haven't gone away and no matter how much they talk about air pollution they haven't been able to do anything about it. They can't seem to put together a public transportation system to help. And no matter how much western slope water they pump over the Divide, they still can't seem to keep their lawns green enough. Given that Denver will probably go bankrupt anyway paying the million dollars a day interest on the new empty airport, I think they should move while they still have traveling money.

If we relocated Denver to Los Angeles, given the current imbalance in population shift from California to Colorado, this move could solve a lot of problems. The Denverites would feel right at home with freeways and smog, and LA wouldn't even notice another million and a half people or so. Then they could leave the mosquitoes alone at Lowry and archaeologists of future millennia could wonder if Denver International Airport was built by space aliens for some kind of weird experiment.

Back to the mosquitoes and the headline. The *Denver Post*, not generally known for its clever headlines, came up with our vote for headline of the week.

"Lowry Mosquitoes Feeding On Red Tape."

July 13, 1994

⋯≡○⊜≡⋯

If Bikers have Changed, What Can We Believe In?

Some good friends in Norwood were having a small party for 50 or so Saturday night. I dragged my wife from milking the goats and we dropped by. It seemed we were among the few that hadn't arrived on a Harley. None of those new yuppie bikes, only ridden by people in Hermes leather, but big mean Harleys. Very large men in black t-shirts and very attractive women in equally black shirts were drinking beer and telling tall tales. In spite of the mellow atmosphere, the sight of some of the colors displayed kept my normally loud opinions muted.

I was thinking that maybe I was in an alien culture, since I was unable to share stories of the old days with them. But then I overheard one conversation that changed everything. He was so big, he could have had an anvil for an earring, and he turned angrily to his ol' lady and said, "The kid is watching entirely too much television; we need to get him to read more, maybe the classics."

Once again my mother's admonition proved true. If you get past outward appearances, people are more the same than they are different. Who knows, maybe someday I can get past dreadlocks.

June 15, 1994

⋯≡○⊜≡⋯

Prairie Dogs and Plague

There's a prairie dog shoot this weekend in Nucla. I plan on going to cover it. Now this year there aren't as many prairie dogs as there have been for previous shoots. It's not that they're over hunted; it's the reverse. The populations of prairie dogs have gotten so thick in recent years that colonies were overlapping. Plague, which is endemic in some prairie dog colonies, spreads through the entire population when there are too many of the critters and they are too close together. I think there may be a lesson in this for people. I am just not sure what it is. That plague is the same one that got 95 percent of the population of much of Europe from 1320 to 1390. But I am not afraid of the plague. My ancestors were among the 5 percent of the population that survived. I'll bet yours were, too.

June 22, 1994

⊷⇒◠⇐⊷

Prairie Dogs and City Rats

The first prairie dog shoot caused considerable commotion on the other side of the mountains. Even the Governor condemned prairie dog shoots, not on moral grounds, but as bad for the tourist economy. He probably forgot that hunters add a few dollars to the economy on this side of the mountains, and most of them don't stay around to build trophy homes.

The leader of the anti-prairie dog shoot protest that first year was from Denver. She told me that it was cruel to kill prairie dogs with a gun, and it was evil to do it for sport. I asked her where she lived. It was in a high rise by Cheesman Park in Denver. I asked her if they had rats in the building. She emphatically told me they did not. I told her that they didn't because part of her condo maintenance fee went to paying the exterminator who poisoned, gassed, and otherwise used cruel and unusual punishments on the rats.

She said that rats carried disease and didn't belong in her building.

I guess we should have named them Prairie Rats. Then it would be OK to gas them and poison them, as long as we didn't have any fun doing it.

If she comes back this year, I really need to show her my plan for reintroducing wolves to Cheesman Park. I wonder if you can control muggers through natural predators. And if they get a few joggers, well, like livestock, they aren't native to this country, nor are they endangered.

June 22, 1994

⋆⟝⊜⟞⋆

Soccer, Not My National Sport

I don't write about sports. There are lots of reasons. Mostly, I'm not very good at it. I'm not much of a fan either. There, I said it. I do watch the Super Bowl faithfully. If you don't watch, you can't have any kind of conversation with anyone the next day, and I'd miss that. I like to go to baseball games occasionally, but I think they are kind of dull on the tube. Having lived in North Carolina for quite some time, I feel obligated to watch the Final Four, but that is about the extent of it. Now comes soccer. The World Cup. Fifty thousand fans flew over from Ireland just to support their team. Brazil declared a national holiday so everyone could watch the games on big screen TVs, partially funded by the government. There was some comment in the press that America has no equivalent of national pride in a truly national team.

Well, I suppose if you have little else to be proud of, perhaps a country should field a World Cup team. The national pride that many countries feel in their World Cup teams is manifest in fans rioting and killing each other en masse at games. Now they have taken it one better. The fans in Columbia murdered one of their players. Andres Escobar, 27, was shot 12 times in a parking lot in Medellin, Columbia Saturday. He had been the most popular member of the team and a national celebrity in Columbia until he accidentally kicked the ball into his own goal, contributing to Columbia's 2-1 upset loss to the United States last week. One of the gunmen is reported by police to have said, "Thanks for the [one] goal." The World Cup governing organization (FIFA) said that things had been going pretty well until then: there had only been two fan riots and one drug scandal. The Columbian coach and his family are in hiding with police protection after a series of graphic death threats.

I would compare this performance with Denver fans and the Broncos. When the Broncos would return from their inevitable Super Bowl losses, the fans would be at the airport and would cheer them. Not to embarrass them, but to make them feel better. They had a parade for them one year after a particularly bad time. Win or lose, they are Denver's team. Lest you think this is strictly the tenacity of Denver fans, it is not unique in America. I remember the New York Mets losing enough games in their first two years to set a record that would never be topped. Nonetheless, New Yorkers, oft accused of a certain lack of compassion, bought out every seat in the stadium and cheered anything the team did right, no matter how seldom they did anything right.

In a time of commercialized sport and multi-million dollar corporate teams, in a time when people bemoan a lack of values in America, one of the great values that survives, in at least a large portion of the fans, is sportsmanship. There is little of that in evidence at the World Cup. On Monday, the highly favored Brazilian team eked out a 1-0 win over the U.S. I shudder to think what would have happened to them if they had lost.

July 6, 1994

⋆⇒◦⇐⋆

Sometimes Getting the Terminology Right is the First Step towards a Solution

Everyone is writing about homelessness and the homeless of late. We looked the term up in the dictionary. It said, "adj. Having no home or haven. n. People without homes considered as a group." Based on current, conventional wisdom, the group called homeless has increased geometrically in recent years. A visit to any major city finds large numbers of the un-housed in parks, doorways and shelters. Far more people than were visible a generation ago. Telluride has been calling its car campers and tent campers and tree house campers homeless, and is no more able to find them conventional homes than San Francisco or Detroit has been able to house its homeless. State and Federal initiatives have been equally unsuccessful in solving this crisis.

Talk show expert guests have defined and redefined the homeless. (Now there's a career, *expert guest*. I wish Oprah had asked me.)

When I was growing up in New York City, many more years ago than I care to remember, there were very few homeless. There were a lot of guys who drank muscatel wine all day and lived under the elevated train tracks in a section called the Bowery, but they weren't homeless, they were winos. My mother told me so, and said it happened to people who didn't go to school and study hard. There were people who slept in doorways at night in the East Village and talked loudly to themselves all day, but they weren't homeless, they were crazies. There weren't many crazies on the streets; most of the crazies were warehoused in large mental hospitals. Every state in the union had huge institutions keeping the mentally ill off the streets. When budgetary constraints made states close these institutions, it put thousands of people who were unable to care for themselves on the streets. The experts came up with a theory of community care to justify closing the hospitals, but community care turned out to be living on the street and competing for handouts from the community.

Before you jump up and tell me that this is an economic problem of the rich getting richer and the poor getting poorer, we need to look at some statistics. In 1959, when America was at the height of prosperity and the homeless had not taken over the cities, 22.4 percent of the population was below the poverty level. The poverty level in 1959 was defined as $2,973 per year for a non-farm family of four. In 1990, 13.5 percent of the population was below the poverty level, and the level was defined as $13,359 per year. The source for these figures is the U.S. Bureau of the Census, *Current Population Reports,* pp. 60-181.

What about the real homeless — the family that has lost their home from loss of job, loss of wage earner, the incredible expense of catastrophic illness? These people need to be helped. As a compassionate society, we are compelled to help our neighbors through their time of need. But applying the politically correct terminology of homelessness to the winos and the crazies has lumped the truly homeless, who we can and should help, into a mass that we can neither help nor embrace into our communities.

It is a frightening concept to "have no home or haven." Small programs to provide job counseling, temporary loans for rent and utility deposits, day care for single parents have proved remarkably successful in many areas. They should not be lost in the rhetoric of civil rights discussions about a wino's right to sleep in the public library or a crazy's right to accost you on the street with demands for a handout.

July 20, 1994

⟡

How Bad Is It? Not as Bad as You Think.

This is sort of an old fashioned newspaper. We try to record the events of our area as the small town chronicles of a half-century ago did theirs. Even stylistically, both in writing and graphics, we have attempted to give the feeling of times past. Long narrow columns of type as you have seen on these pages are from another era of newspaper design. If that gives anyone the idea that we somehow long for simpler times, we do. However, that doesn't mean that we believe that America in the '90s is on the way down or that everything is going to hell in a hand basket in this day and age.

The age of television news and talk shows has brought street crime from far away cities into our living rooms to such an extent that most of us believe that civilization is breaking down. People wringing their hands that compulsive-obsessive Japanese children are spending their lives in the most boring schools in the world learning how to out-compete our children and the general belief that America doesn't produce anything but politicians and lawyers is depressing everyone. It is time to dispel some of those myths.

In the first six months of this year, felonies decreased in almost all of the nation's largest cities. Murder, robbery and assault declined 25 percent in San Francisco compared with the first six months of last year, and were down over 15 percent for Seattle, Los Angeles, El Paso and San Antonio. New York City had a decrease of nearly 10 percent and only two major cities had increases, Phoenix 11 percent and Baltimore 3.2 percent. According to Mark Moore, a criminologist at Harvard

University, "It is good news, but there is so much anxiety about crime that it will take years of statistical declines before anyone believes them." Well, we told you here first, crime rates are going down. In Colorado, serious crime went down 2.6 percent in the second quarter of this year, continuing a downward trend that began more than a decade ago.

After crime, everyone worries about the economy. American manufacturing output last year was 39 percent higher than it was in 1980. It was 95 percent higher than it was in 1970. And as for productivity, we produced all this bounty with only 18.2 million manufacturing workers, compared with 19.3 in 1970. This greater efficiency did not create huge unemployment as some predicted, but released more of the manufacturing force to produce other things we want, from TV mini-series to health care.

The quality of education is a subject that doesn't lend itself to perfect measurement. There is not room here to go through the litany of college-board test scores or the horror stories of illiterate college freshmen. I suspect that the tests are different enough year to year that they are not an adequate measure of change and that there are more college freshmen that are highly literate than are not. Two things stand out however. In 1900, 4 percent of the U.S. population graduated high school. In 1940, 25 percent of the population completed high school. In 1992, 80 percent of the population completed high school and 44 percent attended college. What an incredible improvement. How did they do? Well, between 1976 and 1991, Americans won 62 percent of the Nobel prizes; Britain and Germany were next closest with 8 percent each.

Of late we've made some strides in cleaning up the environment. Lead emissions are down 97 percent since 1970; particulates in the air have dropped 60 percent and hydrocarbons 38 percent. Homes built in 1990 used 30 percent less energy than homes built in the '50s. Cars averaged 21.7 m.p.g. in 1991, up from 13.5 m.p.g. in 1970.

All that is interesting, but what about the breakdown of families? For all the talk, 70 percent of children under 18 live with both parents. The number of divorces has actually dropped from the peak year, 1981, from 1,213,000 to 1,167,000. That is still a lot, but the trend is down. Births by teens, having increased each year from 1986 through 1991, have dropped 2 percent in 1992 and 1993 respectively. Casual drug use is down significantly among teenagers. In 1979, 23 percent of children under 17 were using drugs. By 1991 that number was down to 13.8 percent.

There are a lot of things wrong in the world, in our country, and in our community. There is an awful lot right as well. If sensational reports fool us into thinking that so much is wrong, that nothing is worth fixing, then we are losing our ability to maintain our country as a place for our children and their children to live. Our best weapon in making things right is knowing that it is not an impossible task. It isn't.

November 16, 1994

Interlude . . .

Timing is everything, they say. I had no sooner arrived in Telluride than I lost the job I came there for and the wife I came there with. I seriously wondered about the type and origin of the next event to contribute to such a positive streak of luck. The Sheridan Bar seemed like a good place to go to sort out how I might avoid what was looking more and more like an inevitable "strike three." To a recent acquaintance, I explained my decision to move back to Southern California.

With a sip of his vodka tonic and a whimsically questioning glance he asked, "Besides the job and the wife, why would you do something so drastic?" His matter-of-fact demeanor caused me to doubt my own thought processes. I expressed to him my desire to make a living that could pay for such simple things in life as say my rent, some groceries, gas for the car, and *his* vodka tonic, perhaps (that got his attention). I even imagined contributing to an actual bank account, where the zeros had other positive digits for friends.

Then came that special logic, the likes of which I had never encountered in my 40-plus years on this earth. With absolute conviction, he explained to me that, for over a hundred years, people had moved to Telluride with nothing and left with a fortune. So, in his reality, I didn't have a problem, and counter to my own sense at the moment, I was in exactly the right place at just the right time. I stayed in Telluride and the person that made it happen, with his fanciful grasp on twisted logic, was Peter Spencer, Telluride's mayor.

For Peter there was always a bit of logic, as well as magic, perpetuated through historical fact. The past, as he saw it, could make the future more understandable. He believed I could stay in Telluride and survive, flourish, perhaps. To prove his point, he lent me an office to work out of and a computer to create my work on. But most of all he made me feel I belonged. Peter introduced me to my first client, a restaurant owner who was willing to trade some very nice meals and a few dollars for advertising that, in turn, would bring in more business. So I went to work. The owner got more business, I got more clients, and Peter got free dinners at his favorite restaurant.

From that moment on I never looked back. I was afraid to.

Peter had a knack for seeing the positives, even through the negatives that periodically materialized in his own life. He had an uncanny way of viewing complex events, concepts and issues in simple, more manageable terms in order to come up with simple, more manageable solutions. It is what made him the unique person he was. Peter's special gifts meshed well with his very public persona, driving him to run for mayor, keeping him in a seemingly perpetual conversation on the streets, in the offices and shops and in the bars of Telluride, and causing him, finally, to dream of publishing his own newspaper.

As fate would have it, the journalistic dream of his did come true, so that even those who never had the opportunity to meet him could know this very special individual, his character, imagination and strength through the words he left behind.

Peter Spencer was responsible for introducing me to some of the most incredible people — many of whom are present in these pages — who are fortunately still part of my life. But most of all he showed me as no other person could what constitutes a true friend.

As it all turned out, timing *is* everything, and mine couldn't have been better.

— *Glenn Herbert*

Sooner or Later, Reality Sets In. Sometimes When Least Expected.

I admit it. When the lotto prize starts climbing over several million, I buy some quick picks. When it gets up to eight or ten million, I buy even more quick picks and I notice a lot of people I know doing the same thing. It is probably a relatively harmless habit if it doesn't get out of hand. That is relatively speaking, of course. The Wharton School did research on the effect of gambling on retail sales. The study found that in the test areas, when lottery jackpots were high, retail sales of merchandise were lower. People were spending money on lotto tickets that they would otherwise have spent on merchandise. In case you think that it was trading one luxury for another, sales were equally affected in grocery stores. The research found a similar correlation in areas with racetracks with pari-mutuel betting. There was a direct decrease in retail sales during race meets.

Everyone knows that too much gambling is bad for their family's economic well-being. It isn't good for the economy as a whole. Money and effort that could have gone into the production of goods and services is spent on a game of chance. Borrowing money to gamble is even worse. No bank in their right mind would loan money to you to buy a lotto ticket, and dealing with loan sharks can be injurious to the kneecaps.

Amazingly, if the stakes are high enough and if you change the name of the gambling to derivative investing, the banks will loan money and you may even get invited to make a speech at the Rotary Club on investment strategy. That is exactly why Orange County, California, one of the nation's richest counties, went bankrupt December 6.

In nearly every newspaper account of the financial disaster in Orange County, the reporter said something to the effect that "even experts do not fully understand derivatives." The unsaid conclusion was that the reader was too inexpert and too unsophisticated to understand and the reporter was relieved of any obligation to try to explain what happened. I imagine that was how the Orange County Treasurer, Robert Citron, convinced the County Board to let him bankrupt them. "This sophisticated financial stuff is too complicated for the board, just trust us experts to make you a lot of money."

Well, it isn't that complicated. The reason that the "experts" — those making their living selling leveraged derivatives — don't want to explain it is that, once explained, they become obvious for what they are, shills in a high stakes game. No science, no underlying production, no services, just gambling, and a cut of the gambling pot, commissions for those who told you that it was too complex to understand.

You don't believe us? Think we're exaggerating? We'll prove it. We will explain what happened in Orange County and we bet you'll understand it better than Mr. Citron, better than the Orange County Board, and better than the banks that loaned them their gambling stake.

Not satisfied with investing the county's excess funds in Treasury Bills, or highly rated bonds or insured bank certificates to earn interest, Mr. Citron bet nearly all of Orange County's money that interest rates would go down. Winning the bet would earn far more than conventional investments, and no one considered the possibility of losing. If you think interest rates will go down, you put your money in something long term. Something that will still pay today's higher rates after interest rates drop. That is pretty conventional. But Orange County leveraged that bet. They could borrow from banks at a lower rate than they would get on long-term bonds, so they did. They borrowed 1.2 billion dollars and put it in long-term bonds at higher interest rates. Now they were making money on money they had borrowed.

As we all know, interest rates went up, not down. They now had to pay more interest to the banks than they were earning on their long-term investments. Worse yet, the current value of their long-term bonds dropped because they were no longer paying rates above the current rates. If they sold them, the sales price would not be enough to repay the bank loans. The banks got nervous and called the loans. The county declared bankruptcy. That was the leveraged part.

The derivatives part wasn't so complicated either. A derivative is defined in the financial dictionary as a "financial contract whose value is derived from another investment." It is a bet as to how another investment will do. If you buy a bond for $90, a change in interest rates could make it worth $100 or $80 depending on the direction of the change. If you invest in the derivative — "interest rate futures" — for $90, you are betting that the rates will go up or down. If you lose, you don't have something of less value, you don't have anything at all. You could make $180 on your bet, or lose the whole thing. Not satisfied with the leverage, Orange County invested one-third of their money in an interest rate derivative called an "inverse floater." They bet wrong and lost most of their money. Fancy names don't make a gambling wager into an investment. What is happening in Orange County now? With the money they have left over, they're paying lawyers to explain to them how they betrayed the public's trust instead of paying road crews to patch the potholes and custodians to care for their buildings.

Colorado has laws against local governments doing this sort of thing. These are good laws. We won't make the mistakes they made in California.

By the way, can you loan me five bucks for a lotto ticket?

December 21, 1994

─◦═◑ ◖═◦─

What is About the Price of a New Car, but You Can't Drive It, Live in It, or Pay for the Kids' College with It

Worrying about how to pay your holiday bills? Here is one you haven't received yet. Your share of the national debt is $18,085.

The national debt has climbed by $47,361,000,000 in November. That is 47 billion dollars in one month. It is less than it climbed per month in 1993, but still a considerable number. That brings the total at the end of November to $4,771,162,000,000. That is nearly 5 trillion dollars. If the national debt was a 30 year mortgage at 9 percent interest, the monthly payments would be $38,389,848,543.08. I'm not sure what monthly income you would need to qualify, but I'll bet they would ask for mortgage insurance and a cosigner.

During federal budget hearings over a quarter century ago, a remarkably eloquent Untied States Senator, the late Everett McKinley Dirkson, said, "A billion here and a billion there and soon we're talking about real money." His daughter, Elizabeth, is married to the new Senate Majority Leader, Bob Dole. I hope Elizabeth remembered to tell Bob what her daddy said.

January 4, 1995

·✦═◉═✦·

Did William Randolph Hearst Start This Way?

We were pleased to read that our friends at the *Daily Planet* in Telluride bought the newspapers in Gunnison and Crested Butte as well as the *Shopper* in Montrose. Although they might not agree on the east and west coasts, by San Miguel County standards, that makes them a conglomerate. What with the three sections a week, the Examiners, and a parent company, the *Telluride Times-Journal* ranks as a conglomerate as well.

Here we are, the last of the independent small town papers in San Miguel County. The *Forum* is about as independent as they come, but they're in Montrose County. We were beginning to feel a little like an endangered species. If we were an endangered species, maybe we would qualify for federal aid.

The theory of a conglomerate is that if you know how to run your own business, you also know how to run everyone else's business. Many conglomerates proved, in the '70s and '80s, that wasn't the case. The practice turned out to be that two sick cats don't make a healthy one. However, there is still some appeal to conglomeration. It makes a company less dependent on one source of income. If things go bad in one area, the other areas can make it up. It works sometimes, but the inexorable operation of Murphy's Third Law, "Everything will go wrong at the same time," generally upsets the most carefully crafted conglomerates.

Don't worry about us at *The Post*, however. We have our own conglomerate, right here in Norwood behind Karen's Restaurant. Our chickens produce about four-dozen eggs a day (Spencer's Farm Fresh Eggs from Happy Chickens). We have them on the counter right next to the papers. Most everyone here brings their children to work when they aren't in school. With Amber setting land speed records in her walker, and Cora trying to find a free computer to draw on, and Meghan doing her homework on the roll top desk, and assorted friends and visitors, we could easily be mistaken for a day care center.

We were thinking of renaming the whole operation, *The Norwood Post*, Newspaper, Chicken Farm and Day Care Center (NPNCF&DC Industries). Now that sounds like a conglomerate and we wouldn't be subject to the vagaries of just one source of income.

It didn't work out that way. The first week in January, with everyone broke and recovering from Christmas, advertising revenues were less than terrific. Not much happened as people cranked back up from the holidays and news was hard to come by. Most of the children had colds and stayed home. Counting on the chickens to save the day, we found that they were molting and egg production dropped to half-a-dozen a day. Murphy's Law was in full operation once again. We've almost learned our lesson about operating multiple businesses. We were thinking of opening a fried chicken stand, but the chickens have started laying again.

January 25, 1995

⊷⊜⊶

Renewing Driver's Licenses, Returning Library Books and Renting Videos

There used to be a cartoon character who had a closet full of anxieties. Late at night when he couldn't sleep, a stern looking librarian would appear at the closet door and berate him for not returning an overdue book years before. It didn't help him sleep. I thought of that closet when I finally renewed my expired driver's license last week. I thought I had shut the closet door for a while until I remembered the three rental videos on top of the TV at home accumulating late charges.

I was about to go home and get them when I came across an article in the Wall Street Journal on the video rental industry. It seems that the industry took in 12 billion dollars last year. That included 3 billion dollars in late charges. It made me feel better about the videos. I'll bring them back tomorrow.

March 22, 1995

-*⟩≡⟩◎⟨≡⟨*-

Closing the Gate

Having learned that publishing a weekly newspaper and taking a week off are incompatible, and not having been further than the Wendy's in Montrose for many months, we took a road trip last week. We had been invited to Keystone for a conference on growth in the Rocky Mountain West that was sponsored by the U.S. Forest Service, *Snow Country Magazine*, and the Pinchot Institute. Former Governor Richard Lamm was giving the keynote address, and you can always count on him to make you think and occasionally to offer what many consider shocking solutions to seemingly intractable problems.

It snowed, sleeted, hailed and rained for the three days of the conference, leading us to hope that the next mountain conference will be held at the beach, but Governor Lamm didn't disappoint. He was a three-term governor from 1975 to 1987. Even as Utah is currently waging a massive campaign to bring the Winter Olympics to Salt Lake and has tough competition in the United States and the world, Lamm reminded us that he had waged a successful campaign to keep the Winter Olympics out of Colorado in the late '70s. He is now a college professor at the Center for Public Policy at the University of Denver. As a professor he is even more outspoken, if that is possible. He shares our concerns with population growth, both in Colorado and worldwide.

The Mountain West has added 350,000 people to its existing 12.5 million inhabitants since 1992. There is no end in sight. No, they aren't all from California. It only seems that way. California accounts for 25 percent of the new residents in Colorado and when the economy improves in Colorado and when the economy improves in California, the in-migration will offset much of the out-migration of the last several years. Governor Lamm put the population growth in perspective with some statistics. Africa is the fastest growing continent. It is growing at an annual rate of 2.9 percent. So is Colorado. Our population has averaged 2.9 percent growth for the last five years. It isn't that Colorado's mothers are having babies at a high rate, it is just that nearly everyone wants to live here. Even though *Snow Country Magazine* sponsored the conference, one of the later speakers suggested that every time *Snow Country* or *Outside*, or *Time* runs an article on the "last best places to live," those places become overrun with new residents, and soon everyone is looking for "new last best places."

Governor Lamm pointed out that population growth and economic growth are not twins. Worldwide, the countries with the most stable populations have the highest rates of economic growth. When the oil shale boom hit Colorado (Remember when that was going to make America energy independent? It turned out be another victory of politics over science.), unemployment went up. The boom attracted more new residents than it could employ.

Back in 1790, when they took the first census, the population of the United States was 4 million. Since 1790 the population has doubled 6 times to reach 255 million in 1992. If the population doubles only 2 more times we will have more people than India, more people than China. The birthrate in the U.S. has stabilized. With the current rate, the population will reach 300 million and then hold level. That is, if you leave out immigration. In 1970, immigration to the U.S. was 373,000. In 1990, it was 1,500,000. If the high immigration rate continues, and if the higher birth rates of first generation immigrants continue, then the U.S. population will level out at over 500 million. There are some that might say that we should take a serious look at curtailing immigration. Governor Lamm was one who said it. The reaction ranged from gasps to applause. He does make you think. He made a compelling case. We gave it a lot of thought. I suppose we could change the inscription on the Statue of Liberty to read, "Keep your tired, your hungry, your huddled masses yearning to be free." After all, this country seems pretty crowded with 250 million people. We suppose we could live with another 50 million or so, but another 250 million? That would be just too much. Could you imagine everyone in America twice as close to each other as they are now? We were tempted to stand up and shout, "Right on, Dick, close the gate!"

It was another statistic that kept us from shouting. Since that 1790 census, 56 million people have immigrated to the United States. My grandparents were among them. Unless your ancestors came over on the Mayflower, or you are a full-blooded Native American, your relatives were among those 56 million immigrants. So I didn't shout, "Close the gate." My grandfather would turn over in his grave. But it did make us think. And we aren't sure that we won't shout it sometime, if we think about it long enough.

June 14, 1995

⊷⇒◉⇐⊷

Where have All the Cowboys Gone?

Some years ago we were playing checkers with our daughter. She was seven at the time. The checkers were made of plastic. It was embarrassing to lose consistently to a 7 year old, so we tried to make small talk.

"When I was your age, checkers were made out of wood."

"Were cars made out of wood then, too?" she said innocently. "That must have been the dark ages," she continued, somewhat less innocently. She never lets me forget that exchange and now whenever I mention my childhood, she generally responds, "Was that when cars were made out of wood, dad?"

At that time she wanted to be a paleontologist. A heady career choice for a 7 year old. It was understandable with the childhood fascination for dinosaurs that all of us have shared and many of us have continued into adulthood.

Well, back when cars were made out of wood, we had our career choices, too. They started at an early age with policeman or fireman or cowboy or soldier, and changed to doctor or teacher or author or scientist or senator. Later generations may have substituted astronaut or rock star, and no one wants to be a senator anymore.

We looked at a recent government study undertaken to determine which would be the top jobs for the '90s. It is intended to serve as a guide for career counselors. There were twenty-five on the list. None of our first four choices were included. No policeman or fireman or cowboys or soldiers. There were, however, right there in the top ten, internal auditors, network integration specialists and correctional officers. Will children play "internal auditors and Indians" in the '90s?

The study picked these as the best because they projected high employment and increasing salaries during the '90s. "Mandatory sentencing is expected to increase the demand for correctional officers more than two-thirds over the next decade." Oh boy. "The savings and loan scandal created a boom for internal auditors as more industries step up monitoring on everything from bank deposits to worker efficiency." Sounds like a lot of fun there. It is interesting to note that not a single one of the top twenty-five career recommendations includes a job that produces a product.

Jim Carrier, a fine columnist with the other *Post* newspaper on the Front Range, recently looked at the declining numbers of cowboys in Wyoming. That top career choice of an earlier age is in serious decline. Wyoming, once considered a cowboy state, has 69,484 service workers, 62,093 government workers and only 2,840 full time cowboys. They have another 4,000 seasonal cowboys, but that still gives them ten government workers for every cowboy. The government workers averaged $24,000 per year, the cowboys $6,400.

"No wonder," you say. "There are less cowboys because it is a tough living and you can't make any money."

Well, we have met a few internal auditors who wanted to be cowboys, but never met a cowboy who wanted to be an internal auditor, or a systems integrator, for that matter.

We have spent time studying economics and we keep seeing pronouncements that we now have a service economy. That means that internal auditors and other service workers will dominate the economy. Chauffeuring tourists around, doing their laundry, preparing lawsuits, filling out reports, doing paper work, staring at computer screens will be the economic engine of the future. Frankly, we don't get it.

How does an economy work when we all do each other's taxes and take in each other's laundry and serve each other's food? Who earns the dollars to be taxed in the first place, and who makes the fiber and the laundry detergent and who grows the food? Are we missing something?

The desirability of a life's work is not determined by demand in the job market. There is satisfaction in creating something, whether it is beef on the hoof, or a work of art, or a new septic tank, that goes beyond the job security or the paycheck. There is satisfaction that comes from a teacher or a coach inspiring a student to be their best that is not matched in network integration.

There is satisfaction in creating a newspaper as well. But it takes a lot of staring at computer screens and far too much time indoors. On the front page last week, we had a picture of a cattle drive in the canyon east of Norwood. Hard work and low pay didn't seem to reduce the enthusiasm of the cowboys. We wished we were with them.

Sometimes we wish cars were still made out of wood and children still wanted to be firemen and policemen and cowboys. Some of them still do. And for some it carries over into adulthood. That isn't bad either.

November 15, 1995

⋄⊶⇌⊷⋄

Mother Russia

She was the only one in the gallery without headphones. A round face with snow-white hair wrapped in a babushka sitting in the United Nations gallery among the city folk. While they struggled with the stilted English of the simultaneous translation coming through the headphones, she listened with rapt attention to the eloquent Russian of the Foreign Minister.

The year was 1955. The speaker was Andrei Gromeyko. The woman was Mayna Spevakovsky. She was my grandmother. Her social security card said Mary Spencer, the Americanization that they had given her at Ellis Island in 1905, but one look at that face and you knew she was still Mayna.

She left her beloved mother Russia when the Cossacks burned her home and shop and killed my great grandfather, the rabbi of Katrynislov, a town the family had called home for tens of generations. She never forgave the Tsar for letting the Cossacks ravage in exchange for their support against Lenin and Trotsky.

She outlived her husband by 30 years and lived with my parents the rest of her life. She made us cabbage soup and told us tales of the old country. None of the later generations could speak Russian and she missed the sound of her native tongue. As a child, I would accompany her on the bus to the UN whenever Gromeyko was in town.

Having grown up with the red scares and fallout shelters of the '50s, I asked her once how she could be enthralled with such an evil Communist.

"He was so eloquent and speaks such beautiful Russian," she replied, "that I can forget his politics while I listen to him."

I thought about my grandmother as the returns for the Russian presidential election came over CNN Sunday. There hadn't been an election in Russia in her nine-decade lifetime, or anyone's lifetime, for that matter.

The field for Russian President was crowded. Everything from Communists to free market economists to lunatics.

The country has been involved in a brutal civil war in Chechnya that is as divisive for the Russians as the Viet Nam era was for the United States. As Russia makes the painful transition to a free market economy, their industrial production has fallen by 50 percent, larger than the 35 percent drop in the United States during the Great Depression.

With an arrogance that's difficult to explain, our administration has hinted of dire consequences to American-Russian relations if the people elect anyone but the current President, Boris Yeltzen.

We doubt it has done Yeltzen any good. Clinton's support certainly didn't help Shimon Peres in his losing battle in Israel, and his support of Yeltzen is equivalent to the Russians' of Momar Kadaffi's [sic] support in an American election.

Why did the administration choose to support Yeltzen? Perhaps he fits the American political stereotype; he is a drunk and a lecher. We hope that isn't the reason. It is more likely that the administration, fearing a win by the Communist, worried that it would give Bob Dole a great campaign theme: "The Republicans won Russia from the Communists, Clinton lost it again."

How did the Russian election come out, and what would my grandmother have thought of all this democracy in the land of the Tsars and Commissars?

Yeltzen received 33 percent, the Communist 31 percent, the General 20 percent, and the Economist 8 percent. The rest received negligible votes.

The Russian constitution requires 50 percent plus 1 vote to win. There will be a runoff in thirty days. Yeltzen proved that he had learned much from American politics. On Monday he fired his Defense Minister and appointed the General with 20 percent of the vote as his replacement. On Tuesday he offered the Finance Ministry to the Economist.

There is now no doubt that Yeltzen will sweep the runoff election. There is no doubt that in another burst of arrogance, the Clinton administration will claim a victory for the United States and that the Dole campaign will have to keep searching for an issue that will turn the November election around.

Will a Yeltzen victory continue Russia on the road to a free market economy? Will western style democracy survive in the land of the Tsars and the Commissars? We have no idea. We wish grandmother was still here so we could ask her. The vast lands of Mother Russia are remarkably resilient. In the last three centuries they have survived the invasions of countless enemies. They were invaded by everyone from the Mongols and Japanese to the Prussians and Poles and Germans. They were even invaded by the Swedes.

What would grandmother have said? We think she would have said, "Yeltzen speaks Russian like a peasant. That's good, too."

June 19, 1996

⌁⇒◒⇐⌁

Sometimes, Adventure Finds You

When I got home there was a cross burning on the front lawn. This was not an everyday occurrence, even in York County, South Carolina, a quarter century ago, and why me?

The schools had been integrated for five years and things were going better than they were in Boston. I had had some threats from the Klan when I integrated a textile mill several years before, but I had more serious trouble from the neighbors whose maids we had hired. Anyway, you don't worry about anonymous telephone threats in the night; it's the ones who show up at the door that should be taken most seriously. I still couldn't figure out why they had chosen my house on this quiet evening to advertise their displeasure.

I counted the children and let the dog out. While loading the twelve-gauge with double ought, I called the neighbors. York was a rural agricultural community of peach orchards, grape vines, bean fields and close families. I had two good friends and neighbors, and they were just getting home from work. Neither answered the phone. I looked out the window and LeGrande, the closest neighbor, was coming at a dead run, dressed like Rambo and armed to the teeth. I wondered if he went to work that way.

"Wha'd you do to tick off the Klan, Spence?"

I had no idea.

By then Melvin's pick-up came roaring into the drive. "They've got the wrong house," said Melvin.

"How'd you know, Melvin? You been goin' to their meetings?" LeGrande drawled.

Melvin was chairman of the school board. His family had settled in York some fifty years before the Revolutionary War and he knew everything. He proceeded to explain that the board had voted to integrate the cheerleading squad that very morning. It seems that when they integrated the schools, York's basketball team improved significantly. Within just a few years they were winning the State 2A Championship regularly. No one seemed to mind the integrated team. Even the Klan came to the games. Unfortunately, the white selection committee for the cheerleaders just couldn't find a black girl qualified for the squad. The board, acting with unexpected wisdom, decided to let the black teachers pick half the squad and the white teachers pick the other half. Winning basketball games was one thing, but cheerleaders were something else again. Melvin had gotten three or four death threats at the tractor dealership that very afternoon.

"I'm going to call the sheriff," I said with determination.

LeGrande proceeded to tell me, with some emphasis, that we handled things ourselves in York County. I called anyway.

"Sheriff, there's a cross burning on my lawn and Melvin is getting death threats."

I think sheriffs must be elected for life in South Carolina and I know very little gets them excited. This sheriff was no exception. I expected sirens and police protection. I got advice.

"Boy (he called everyone boy except the mayor), if them boys come over and you have to shoot one or two of them, make sure they fall on your property before you call me."

It was time to listen to LeGrande. We each opened a Pabst Blue Ribbon from the cooler in the back of Melvin's pickup and worked out the strategy. Since we weren't sure if the Klan would get the right house the second time, we would each stay up at our own house all night, armed with coffee and shotguns and rush to the aid of whoever was attacked. I sent the rest of the family for a sleep over and let the dog back in the house.

It was a long night. Sometime near midnight a car drove slowly up the road, turned its lights out about three hundred yards away and coasted to a stop between Melvin's house and mine. This was it.

I heard LeGrande's front door slam and I headed out, gun in sweaty hands. By the time I got to the car, LeGrande had his ten-gauge stuck through the driver's window and Melvin was aiming a pair of 45's at the passenger door.

It wasn't the Klan.

The high school boy and his date were trying unsuccessfully to rearrange their clothes while explaining that they hadn't been doing anything wrong. It took a few minutes to convince LeGrande that they weren't dangerous. Melvin's hysterical laughter helped.

We sent the kids on their way. I don't think they parked anywhere at night for a long time. We all went back to Melvin's house and finished the Blue Ribbon. We figured if anyone else showed up we'd offer them a beer.

The basketball team was beaten in the state finals that year, but the cheerleaders won.

October 2, 1996

Hardly Business as Usual. Peter's mayoral campaign button and business card, proclaiming his personal and professional philosophy.
Image courtesy of Steve Larson

CHAPTER FIVE

A History Lesson . . . from a Fearless Perspective . . . or Stories from a Checkered Past

Preliminaries . . .

Peter Spencer's great big belly laugh is legendary, and it was accompanied by a certain twinkle in his eyes that said he was laughing at even more than what was intended to be funny. He laughed at the absurdities of life and dealt with them in his own inimitable style. Peter adored making fun of people who were too self-absorbed or at things that begged to be taken too seriously. One of his favorite potshots was aimed at the "Telluride Festival Syndrome" and the direction in which it seemed to be heading. Everyone had gotten too big for his (or her) britches and the level of security was beginning to resemble a Telluride Gestapo. Of course, the grandest festival parody of all was the now defunct Gin Festival, which was never announced and took place on someone's vacant lot, not always with their knowledge. Peter happened to be mayor at the height of the Gin Festival's popularity and patronage. Appropriately, Hizzoner opened the festivities by throwing out the first olive. He also exercised his mayoral prerogative and disbanded the town's open container law for one day.

Bill Graham promoted a mid-summer festival in 1991 and Peter was put in charge of backstage security. The ranks and files of previous Telluride security teams were aghast when Peter assigned the single most important security spot of all — the stairs leading to the stage — to none other than myself, all five foot two inches of me. That was Peter thumbing his nose as only he could do.

Many years back I owned a 1985 Ford Van, and if I do say so, it was a rather well known and easily recognizable landmark around town. The van was decked out like disco. When I decided to sell it, Peter and I conspired to have "Bobbie's Disco-Van Retirement Festival". Peter created 100 laminates, mimicking the VIP laminates that were issued for the various Telluride festivals. But instead of backstage passes, Peter created backseat passes, and issued them to 100 of our best friends. We hired a driver and bartender and basically drove around the town loop, over and over again, stopping at all of the bars to let in those people with backseat passes and drop off those who had had enough. Peter personally ran security for this one, manning the van's sliding door all night long. By the way, he was still mayor at the time.

Perhaps most of all, Peter and I shared a love of history, particularly Telluride history. We were teammates year after year during the annual Telluride Trivia Contest, a fundraiser for the Telluride Historical Museum. Peter and I were just about equals when it came to history recall, the difference being that I had studied and crammed for weeks in preparation. He never cracked a book. The questions were tough and we were good, but it was always the final Grand Bonus lucky guess question — which invariably had something personal to do with one of the judges seated before us — that killed us. One of Peter's and my pet peeves was the telling of inaccurate history, such as the date attributed to William Jennings Bryan's "Cross of Gold" speech on the big rocks near Elk's Park, or the misnomer "Miner's Hospital" when referring to the old Telluride Hospital (now the Telluride Historical Museum). These blunders and oversights used to drive us crazy, so we set out to "re-write" Telluride history — and we did. But we never won that damn trivia contest.

— *Bobbie Shaffer*

Hey, Mr. President, Wanna Buy a Good Used Car?

There wasn't a gate on the White House driveway until 1938. Too many cars were driving up to the portico by then to take a look, so they finally installed a gate and gatekeeper. Even in the summer of 1941, with talk of war everywhere, Washington D.C. was still a sleepy southern town. You didn't need a pass to get on the While House grounds, and government clerks in those days before air-conditioning would take brown bag lunches and sit on the lawn to eat. In December of that year, it would change forever. The morning after the Japanese attacked Pearl Harbor, the head of the Secret Service started looking for a bulletproof car for President Roosevelt. He ran into a federal law that said that no government agency could spend more than $750 for an automobile. Even in those days, that didn't buy an armored limousine.

To his credit, rather than try to circumvent the law, he started looking for some vehicle that the government already owned. The Treasury Department, under which the Secret Service operated, had in storage the perfect limousine. When they had convicted Al Capone on tax evasion charges, the Treasury had seized his bulletproof Packard limousine. The agent in charge had it washed and lubed and brought it around to the White House that afternoon. He asked the President what he thought, and Roosevelt is reported to have said, "I don't think Al would mind."

The President used the car for the next three years, until Ford Motor Company, unhappy that the chief executive was driving around in a competitor's car, built him a new one. They got around the purchase restriction by leasing it to the Secret Service for $500 per year.

It is hard to envision the director of the Secret Service or anyone else in Washington suggesting that the President drive around in a used car today. But other things changed in those days as we were on our way to the huge Washington bureaucracy that we live with today. The government collected about five billion dollars in taxes in 1940. By 1945 it was collecting fifty billion dollars a year. The money was needed for the war effort, and it was a time [when] people were willing to sacrifice, but the number never got lower after the war was over.

Did you ever wonder how the tax rates could go up ten times and everyone still be able to pay them and not have a revolution? A New York department store executive came to Washington with a new concept that the government started in the early years of the Second World War. It was the installment plan for paying taxes.

Until 1942, you paid income taxes the next year on your previous year's earnings, much as property taxes are paid today. It was a real hardship if you lost your job or retired, paying taxes on last year's higher earnings with this year's lower earnings, but tax rates were low and there was only the normal groaning. With taxes more than doubling every year during the war, there was no way the people could pay their previous year's taxes unless they were staunch savers, something that has never been common in America.

Now along comes the Treasurer of Macy's with a plan. He had helped make Macy's one of the great retailing giants by refining lay-away plans and making installment buying a way of life. He proposed that the government forgive all of last year's taxes so no one had to pay two years at once and start deducting this year's taxes weekly from everyone's paycheck. Most people were for it because they thought they were skipping a year's taxes. Of course they would never see the savings until the year after they quit work or retired or died. The government was for it because the taxes they collected currently would be more than they would have collected the old way, what with higher rates and more people working. It was like a forced savings plan, only you made the deposits and the government made the withdrawals. It worked so well for the government that the system continues today.

The ability to make unlimited withdrawals on the deposits of 120,000,000 working people probably explains why the President doesn't drive around in a used limo anymore, and why every member of Congress is provided, at no cost to them, better health insurance than we can ever afford for ourselves.

August 31, 1994

◦‑➲◗═◄◦

Where's Old Teddy Roosevelt when We Need Him?

The United States now has some 20,000 troops in Haiti and, although official figures are hard to come by, there are somewhere less than 100 thousand and more than 10 thousand in or on their way to Kuwait. It remains to be seen whether democracy can be given to or imposed on Haiti and whether Aristide will not succumb to the Haitian tradition of declaring himself Presidente a Vie (President for Life) after our troops leave. But at least the Haitians are eating a little better and are less likely to be beaten or shot for the time being. And the Kuwaitis are safe from another Iraqi onslaught, for the time being, and as of this writing we haven't suffered any casualties.

Both of these uses of our forces have justification, but there is a certain irony in our committing troops to restore democracy in Haiti while committing even more troops to defend a feudal monarchy in Kuwait. Things were simpler in 1904. We would only go to war over American interests. That year, we nearly went to war over a single American citizen.

In 1904, Mr. Jon Perdicaris, a wealthy American retiree in Morocco, was kidnapped from the terrace of his summer villa in the hills above Tangier. His kidnapper was Sherif Mulaf Ahmed ibn-Muhammed er Raisuli. The "Raisuli" was an imposing figure (Sean Connery played him in the movie). He was a Berber chief, lord of the Rif and the last of the Barbary Pirates. He hoped to supplant the Sultan of Morocco by proving the Sultan was powerless, even under international pressure, to get Mr. Perdicaris back. He wanted to have Teddy Roosevelt negotiate with him personally. Roosevelt immediately dispatched two squadrons of warships and Marines to Morocco. The demands of the Raisuli were primarily for the Moroccan government to give him the Rif and pay him some money and let him rule most of Morocco. The Sultan of Morocco, not nearly as able a ruler as the Raisuli, refused. As the American squadron sailed into the harbor in Tangier, the U.S. ambassador cabled Roosevelt and his Secretary of State John Hay that an ultimatum to the Moroccan government was needed for them to make a deal with the Raisuli.

The cable arrived on June 21, 1904. It was the first day of the Republican National Convention. Many delegates were not happy with Roosevelt's Presidency. Hunting and exploration took up more time than affairs of state, and as popular as he was with the electorate, most party regulars did not share their enthusiasm. He was going to be nominated the next day, but it was going to be reluctantly.

On the morning of June 22, John Hay cabled the Moroccan government Roosevelt's ultimatum. "This Government wants Perdicaris alive or Raisuli dead!" Two hours later, waving a newspaper headline of the ultimatum over the convention floor, Senator Depew pronounced, "Magnificent, magnificent! The people want an administration that will stand by its citizens, even if it takes the fleet to do it." Within minutes, Roosevelt was nominated by acclamation amid waving flags and handkerchiefs and hurrahs.

It wasn't long before the Moroccan government met the Raisuli's demands and delivered Perdicaris to the fleet, safe and sound. Perdicaris said that this was "such proof of his country's solicitude for its citizens and for the honor of its flag."

Had this happened today, the congressional opposition, the news commentators, the pundits, the experts would have written the whole thing off as a political maneuver of the worst kind by Teddy Roosevelt. But Roosevelt did get an American citizen released by kidnappers half a world away. He got him released quickly and safely. Yes, it helped him with the nomination and with the election that followed. It helped him because it made people proud of their government. That is politics in its best form.

No President could order out the military to save a single citizen today. The advisors and the second guessers and the lawyers and the pollsters and the media consultants would debate the idea to a slow death while the hostage grew old. Roosevelt sent the fleet the same day he got the news. He asked his Attorney General, Philander Knox, if he had the authority to attack Morocco. Knox was used to the President overriding his advice and even admired him for it. He replied, "Ah, Mr. President, why have such a beautiful action marred by any taint of legality?" That statement alone would have probably gotten them both run out of office today.

Looking at history through the nostalgia brought on by current frustration with government is dangerous. Many of the good old days weren't so good. But I do wish I had been there when Roosevelt ordered out the fleet to save one lone American.

October 19, 1994

⟶⟩◎⟨⟵

It's Hard to Write about Politics at Christmas, and Some Youngsters Don't Know about Virginia

The newspaper office tends to fill up with people as we approach deadline. Most have just come to chat and catch up on the latest gossip or fill us in on the juiciest rumor. It is always distracting, but always fun. This week with Christmas approaching, it seemed particularly difficult to get anything written, as the general excitement is everywhere. At some point I made the remark, "Yes, Virginia, there is a Santa Claus." To my utter amazement, two of my young (ok, 25 is young to me) visitors said, "Who is Virginia?"

I thought everyone knew the story of Virginia and her letter to her hometown newspaper in the days when the country's faith in their papers was still absolute. Since not everyone remembers the story, we feel compelled to tell it again, to educate a new generation, and to remind an older one.

In the summer of 1897, there lived a little girl named Virginia O'Hanlon at 115 West 95th Street in New York City. She asked her father, Dr. Phillip O'Hanlon, who was the police surgeon and deputy coroner, if there was a Santa Claus, and if he had ever seen him on Christmas Eve. He said that although he knew there was a Santa Claus, he had never seen him on Christmas Eve. Virginia said that wasn't enough to convince her friends. Her father suggested that she write to the *New York Sun* and let them settle the argument.

Virginia wrote the following letter to the *Sun* on September 21, 1897.

"Dear Editor:

I am 8 years old. Some of my little friends say there is no Santa Claus. Papa says, 'If you see it in the *Sun*, it's so.' Please tell me the truth, is there a Santa Claus?

Viginian O'Hanlon."

The *Sun* replied in an editorial. It read, in part:

"Virginia, your little friends are wrong. They have been affected by the skepticism of a skeptical age. They do not believe except what they see.

"Yes, Virginia, there is a Santa Claus. He exists as certainly as love and generosity and devotion exist. You might get your Papa to hire men to watch in all the chimneys on Christmas Eve to catch Santa Claus, but if they did not see Santa Claus coming down, what would that prove? Nobody sees Santa Claus, but that is no sign that there is no Santa Claus. The most real things in the World are those that neither children nor men can see."

The editorial was unsigned, but most agree that the author was *Sun* editor Francis P. Church. The *Sun* reprinted it every year until 1950. Virginia taught in the public school system in New York until 1959. She died in 1971 at age 82.

We don't know if *The Post* has readers that are as confident in our accuracy as Dr. O'Hanlon was in the *Sun*'s, but for everyone of the Virginias and all of the other children out there, we can say with absolute certainty, "Yes, there is a Santa Claus."

December 21, 1994

⊹⟩⟨⊹

I Knew Harry Truman, and Let Me Assure You, They Are Not Harry Truman

A very long time ago, when I was in college, I met Harry Truman. The former President had come to the school to teach four days of seminars as a guest professor of history. The school was a bastion of conservative thinking. It had, by then, graduated President William Howard Taft, as well as future President George Bush. The *Literary Review* was edited by William F. Buckley, the future editor of the conservative *National Review.* Nixon was Vice-President of the United States, Joe McCarthy had convinced the country that everyone needed to take a loyalty oath, Fidel Castro was hiding in the mountains of Cuba, the New York Yankees won the Series again, Postmaster General Summerfield banned *Lady Chatterley's Lover* from the mail as "smutty," and gasoline was less than 25 cents a gallon.

History has treated Mr. Truman very well. That was later. At the time, he had neither the popularity nor the respect that he is afforded today and he was in for tough questioning and a long four days. Perhaps because I was as out of place there as he was, I had been assigned as his campus guide. It was long before the more imperial presidencies of today. There was not much of an entourage, an occasional reporter and two secret service agents, and they didn't even have radios. He had no staff, and he carried his own briefcase. He would rise, as was his lifelong habit, at 5:30 a.m. and at 6:00 would be out for his brisk morning walk. Even though he was 70 years of age, it was not easy to keep up with him.

At the first seminar he conducted, it was for senior history majors, he was asked why he had brought the bulk of the army home from Europe soon after VE Day in 1945. Why hadn't he used the army to prevent the Soviet Union from taking over Eastern Europe or even used it to invade Russia and kick Stalin out? Truman took a well-worn copy of the *Chicago Tribune* out of his equally well-worn briefcase. *The Tribune*, along with many other major papers, was calling for Truman's impeachment, only months after the end of the War in Europe, for not bringing the troops home soon enough. Only the hindsight of the next decade could have had anyone thinking that the American people would have let him do anything else.

The next question was even more telling. "Mr. Truman, how difficult was it to decide to drop the atomic bomb on Hiroshima and Nagasaki?" Before we discuss the answer, let us jump to the present. It is now fifty years since the B-29 Super-fortress called the Enola Gay was used to drop an atomic bomb on Hiroshima, the decision that ushered in the nuclear age. The Smithsonian Institution had planned to have an exhibit of the Enola Gay during this fiftieth anniversary. Historians at the Institution, born a decade after the war ended, had written a script for the exhibition. Using a multi-cultural filter of the 1990s, and ignoring the brutal Japanese invasions of Korea, Manchuria and China in the 1930s, the exhibit was to describe the Second World War in the Pacific as "a war of the Japanese people trying to maintain their cultural identity." The script also said that casualty estimates for an invasion of Japan were largely overestimated by the military in an attempt to get revenge for Pearl Harbor. The lowest estimates by Truman's military staff for an invasion of the Japanese home islands were 250,000 American dead and 300,000 wounded. The staff estimated 500,000 Japanese dead and nearly 1,000,000 wounded. Several Smithsonian historians said that there would only be 63,000 Americans dead, and the loss of 80,000 lives at Hiroshima wasn't worth it. Considering that the Marines took 35,000 casualties in the 36 days of fighting on Iwo Jima, a very small island, and that 100,000 Japanese and 13,000 Americans were killed on Okinawa, those estimates seem quite low. Historian Samuel Eliot Morrison has noted that Japan still had "more than 5,000 airplanes with kamikaze-trained pilots and a million ground troops prepared to contest every beachhead and every city." Would they have surrendered without the bomb? No one can know. But they had sworn to fight to the death. Throughout the war the Japanese troops almost universally preferred death in combat or suicide to surrender. There were about 5,000 Japanese defenders at Tarawa. Only three surrendered. The war was not a clash of cultural identity; it was a struggle of good and evil. In the last year of the war, 10,000 Americans died in Japanese prisoner of war camps.

Well, veteran's groups were incensed over the proposed Smithsonian script, and museum officials were incensed over anyone interfering with their revised history. What did Harry Truman have to say about the issue? He did as he always had, took responsibility and told it like it was. In answer to the question of how difficult it was to drop the bomb, Truman said, "It was far from my most difficult decision. After listening to everyone, and looking in my own heart, I knew that anything that would shorten the war and save hundreds of thousands of our sons' and daughters' lives was the only choice that I could make. I alone made the decision. It was right then and it is right now." What did the Smithsonian do? They decided that any discussion of the events leading up to the dropping of the bomb at the end of the war was too controversial. They have decided to just show the bomber and say that it dropped the bomb.

Harry Truman always said that he didn't give 'em hell. "I just tell it like it is and they think it's hell."

We miss you Harry, especially at the Smithsonian.

February 8, 1995

-◇≡◯═◇-

Good Old Days

There is a yearning in much of the populace to return to the good old days in America. Less crime, less poverty, more education, more traditional families, less government. That yearning has been reflected in the political rhetoric of both parties. Newt Gingrich has been referring to life in the '30s and '40s as reflected in movies like *Boy's Town* and *It's a Wonderful Life* as models for present day society. It is a tempting idea. Especially for those too young to remember the good old days or those who have forgotten them. There is certainly much to be admired in decades past, but we should not be too quick to trade.

To give some perspective to the good old days, we will take a trip back to 1940. It is a little more than half a century ago. It was 11 years after the Stock Market Crash of 1929 and a year before the United States' entry into World War II. The 1940 census showed the population to be 132 million. Most demographers agreed that the number wouldn't get much larger. Nine million men were unemployed. There weren't reliable figures kept on women's unemployment: 83 percent of married women did not have jobs outside the home. Three million men were working for the WPA and 30 percent of all black families were on relief.

The country had its first peacetime draft, but nearly half of the men called up did not pass their physicals. The largest single cause was the lingering effects of childhood malnutrition. There was no school lunch program then, nor aid to dependent children. According to the 1940 census, over half the families with children had annual incomes of less than $1,500. The average farmer had an income of $1,000 per year.

There was one phone for every seven Americans. The rate is now one to one. That may or may not be progress. Rural electrification had succeeded in bringing electricity to one in every four farms. A little more than half of all homes had flush toilets. Only three out of four had running water. The average student completed eight years of school before dropping out.

So what, you say. Things aren't as good as they were 20 years ago. Maybe we improved our lot since 1940, but since the early '70s everything has been going backwards. Conventional wisdom tells us that we are not as well off as we were a decade or two ago. National leaders of both parties and just about everyone else believes we are losing ground. When President Clinton launched his campaign in 1991, he stated his theme, "Middle class people are bringing home a smaller paycheck to pay more for health care and housing and education." That theme has been central to both parties and has struck a responsive chord in the electorate. The trouble is that it is simply not true. Personal income, adjusted for inflation, is five times what is was in 1940. True, the growth rate has slowed since the early '70s, but it is still growing. Comparing workers with roughly the same job in 1970 to 1990, if the 1970 worker could afford the then average 1,200 square foot house, the 1990 worker could afford the now average 2,200 square foot house. You may be paying more for health care, but the care is better. The proof is that your child's life expectancy is four years longer than it would have been 20 years ago. It is true that for the lower end of the middle class many higher paying, lower skilled jobs have disappeared, and formerly reliable middle-level positions have been jeopardized by corporate reorganizations. These are problems that must be solved through better education and job training, but the great American Middle Class is still gaining in real income, even if at a slower rate than in the heady years of the '50s and '60s.

Many economists believe that the country may be on the verge of bursting out of two decades of slow growth. The downsizing and computerization and automation of the last decade may be about to create a period of sustained economic growth. Given economic growth and the American talent for problem solving, the future can hold much more promise than the past.

March 22, 1995

⋅→⫘◉⫘←⋅

The Facts Ma'am, Just the Facts

We have never seen a television series with a history teacher as the central character. When *L. A. Law* was at the top of the ratings, law school enrollments went up. It remains to be seen what that televised murder trial in California, whose name we have promised never to mention in print, will do to law school enrollments. We think they will go down significantly. Some years ago, every high school advisor thought that their students should go to engineering school, the jobs [with] the highest salaries when you graduated. Then it was computer science: "America is facing a shortage of computer scientists — study it and you will always have a job." The career of the year this year is environmental science. As with other popular courses of study, the field has become over-crowded, and we are anxiously awaiting the next trend. The teaching of history has never been trendy. The closest we have seen is Shelby Foote narrating the fine series on the Civil War on PBS, but he will never inspire a rush to history classes in the way that *ER* or *Chicago Hope* has inspired a rush to pre-med courses or *Baywatch* will inspire visions of a career as a lifeguard. The teaching of history is the noblest of professions. In spite of that nobility, it is neither attracting the quality nor the quantity of educators that are required to give the coming generations the background that they need to understand the modern world. We suppose it has something to do with the prestige or the money that is associated with a career in history. A typical question to an applicant for a high school history teaching job is, "Can you coach JV football as well?"

Why is the study of history, largely relegated to the sidelines today, so important? It probably won't get you a better job. It certainly will not make you more popular among your peers, nor will it make you the center of attention at parties. It will, however, give you a framework from which to put current events into perspective. There is so much concern about homelessness and the effects that the homeless are having on our central cities. Homelessness is largely viewed as a problem unique to this decade. Any good course in modern American history would teach about the tens of thousands of homeless families that migrated from the dust bowl of Oklahoma to the promised land of California in the thirties only to be turned away by armed men at the state line. Then there were the 25,000 or so penniless World War I veterans who camped with their wives and children in the parks of Washington D.C. in that desperate summer of 1932, waiting for a bonus that never came. President Hoover locked himself in the White House and refused to meet with them. He eventually sent Army Chief of Staff MacArthur to remove them. Troops burned them out and used tear gas to disperse the women and children.

There is a general belief that politics is not only a dirty business, but that it is getting immeasurably worse. Dirty tricks started with Nixon's second campaign and it has been all down hill from there. No one is interested in issues; it is scandal and sound bites that make a campaign. A careful reading of political history will probably convince everyone that the dirtiest campaign in America was the presidential election of 1800. Newt Gingrich may have called the first lady a nasty name, but when President John Adams was facing a serious challenge from Thomas Jefferson, he called him an atheist and an adulterer. Not to be outdone, Jefferson announced that Adams had sent an envoy to London, at government expense, to procure four prostitutes for White House entertainment. Then there was President Warren G. Harding, who accepted cash bribes right in the Oval Office.

Now, don't think that we only view history as a litany of the bad things to show that things aren't so bad by comparison. It may be incorrect in the current atmosphere of blamelessness that seems to permeate social thought in this decade, but there are and have been genuine bad guys throughout history. In many cases, America has risen to the occasion and fought the bad guys on principle alone. When the Marines of our young country put the Tripoli pirates out of business nearly two hundred years ago and our government proclaimed, "millions for defense, but not one cent for tribute," we were at our finest. If everyone knew that one hundred years later Teddy Roosevelt was willing to go to war with Morocco over a single American hostage, perhaps we would have handled modern hostage situations a little bit differently.

There is so much more to be learned from the history of our country and the world. The teaching of history should not be diluted with the social fluff of this decade. It is a subject of facts and of dates and of people. If we do not understand history, we are doomed to repeat its worst mistakes. The teaching of history will not come into vogue any time soon, we think, but it should.

July 12, 1995

-+⟹⟸+-

Counting the Years

In about 1,600 days it will be December 31, 1999. Of course that won't be the turn of the century. The first century obviously ended with the year 100, so the twentieth must end with the year 2000 and we will celebrate on December 31, 2000. That is, unless you think that there was a year zero or that a baby is 1 year-old at birth. The other problem is what to call the next decade. This decade is obviously the nineties; will the next one be the "oughts?" This discussion was held on December 31, 1899. Some disagreed, but mathematics eventually won the day, and the country, except for a few diehards, celebrated the dawn of the twentieth century on December 31, 1900.

It was a time of great optimism for the future. The *New York Times,* ignoring the mathematics, reported on December 31, 1899, "We step upon the threshold of 1900 which leads to the new century facing a still brighter dawn of civilization." The *Boston Herald* thought, "If one could not have made money this past year, his case is hopeless." The *Louisville Courier-Journal* reported, "Business in Louisville was never better, if as good." Not to be less optimistic, the *Cheyenne Sun Leader* said, "Never has a year been ushered in with more promise."

No wonder the country was optimistic. There had been a major recession in 1894-95. It was over and the country was booming. Steel production had doubled; coal production was setting new records. The inventions of the last half of the nineteenth century were bearing fruit. The steam engine, railroads, the telegraph, the telephone, electric lights, the caterpillar tractor were all changing the nation. Business was booming. The motorcar was beginning to make its presence felt. The first car built for sale in the United States was bought in 1898. By 1900 there were 9,000 cars in the country and New York City boasted 100 taxis. Predictions for the motorcar were especially promising. One editorial reported, "It is hardly possible to conceive the appearance of a crowded wholesale street in the day of the automotive vehicle. In the first place, it will be almost as quiet as a country land — all the crash of horses' hoofs and rumble of steel tires will be gone. And since vehicles will be fewer and shorter than the present team and truck, streets will appear less crowded."

The portly, affable William McKinley was the President, and the public could stop by the White House on tour and shake his hand. He had a strong sense of propriety. He once told a photographer, "We must not let the young men of the country see their President smoking." The world was at peace and would stay that way, more or less, for fourteen more years.

The turn of the century was a good time for America. It wasn't that there weren't any problems. There was the battle for women's suffrage to be won. There were the intolerable working conditions for children to be eliminated; there was poverty and injustice and disease to be cured. In less than a year President McKinley would lie dead at the Buffalo Exposition, [the victim] of an assassin's bullet. The San Francisco earthquake was only six years away, followed by the panic of 1907, which brought the nation's banks to the brink of ruin. What made the turn of the century a good time for America was that the vast majority of the people were optimistic. They believed that the country could solve any problem if they set their minds and their energies to it. In large measure, they could.

Just three years later, the Wright brothers took off from the sand dunes of Kitty Hawk, North Carolina. San Francisco came back from the earthquake bigger and better. Within a decade, the great white fleet had established America as a force in the world. Women achieved universal suffrage by 1912, and the two million children from 10 to 15 years old working in factories were freed in 1913. The First World War would follow, but the optimism would not be lost for years to come.

The insecurities of the current age are themselves breeding a disposition towards failure. Doomsayers to the contrary, the problems facing the nation are no greater and no less than the country has faced in the past. Without the belief that a determined people can overcome the problems of the age, there will be no solutions.

On the New Year's Eve that started this century, United States Senator Chauncey Depew said, "There is not a man here who does not feel 400 percent bigger in 1900 than he did in 1896, bigger intellectually, bigger hopefully, bigger patriotically, bigger in the breast from the fact that he is a citizen of a country that has become a world power for peace, for civilization and for the expansion of its industries and the products of its labor." We hope that we can truthfully echo the words of Senator Depew five years from now when the ball on Times Square drops to signal the start of the new millennium.

July 26, 1995

-*≫◉☜*-

An Unsettling History of Welfare

1932 was the cruelest year. The stock market was worth just 11 percent of its value of three years before. The country's Gross National Product had fallen from 104 billion dollars to 41 billion. That year, 273,000 families were evicted from their homes and the average weekly wage for those who had jobs was $16.31. 86,000 businesses had closed their doors and 5,000 banks had failed.

Men had been raised to believe that if you worked diligently, you would succeed. Failure was dragging down the diligent and the shiftless alike. President Herbert Hoover's campaign slogan was, "A chicken in every pot and two cars in every garage." The reality was echoed in the hit song of the year. Rudy Vallee sang, "Once I built a railroad, made it run. Made it race against time. Once I built a railroad, now it's done. Brother, can you spare a dime?"

Somewhere between 15 million and 17 million jobless families declared themselves penniless. They then had a chance of going on relief, the welfare of the day. That did not count the 11 million farm families for whom no statistics were kept. Beef was bringing two and a half cents a pound; wheat was 25 cents a bushel, and a bushel of oats, a dime. With interest running at $3.60 an acre and taxes $1.90, a wheat farmer would lose $1.50 on every acre he reaped, and a wagonload of oats couldn't buy a pair of shoes.

If you declared yourself penniless and went on relief, you had only a one in four chance of receiving any help. When help was given it was very small. A family of four in Philadelphia would receive $5.50 per week, in New York $2.39 and in Detroit 60 cents. The New York City Health Department reported that over 20 percent of the pupils in the public schools were suffering from malnutrition. The *New York Herald Tribune* reported in September of that terrible year, *A teacher suggested that one little girl go home and eat something, the child replied, "I can't. This is my sister's day to eat."*

These are the good old days for which we have little nostalgia. Let us jump to the present. Senator Lauch Faircloth, Republican of North Carolina and Senator Phil Gramm, Republican of Texas, have proposed a bill to end 150 anti-poverty programs, among them food stamps. Their bill has the backing of 24 other Republican Senators.

"Wait," you say, "you set us up with that story. Welfare is a huge part of our budget deficit. Your stories are from the Depression. Deserving people couldn't get good jobs. Besides, welfare mothers have babies to get more money, once people get on welfare they never get off the dole, welfare fraud is rampant, we can't afford the cost, and besides they are all minorities and illegal immigrants. They are living very well on our tax dollars. Welfare is destroying the country."

If we believed all that we would probably vote for the Faircloth/Gramm Bill. The trouble is that none of those common beliefs are true.

First, welfare is not a huge part of our budget deficit. Welfare payments represent about 1 percent of the budget. Medicare is 11 percent, Social Security is 22 percent and Defense and the interest on the National Debt are even higher proportions of our budget.

As for welfare mothers having more babies to get more money, there have been several highly publicized cases, but the fact is that most welfare families are small. The average number of children in a family receiving Aid to Dependent Children nationally is 2.9. In Colorado the typical welfare recipient has one or two children, the same as the rest of the families in the state. And most don't stay on welfare. In Colorado, the typical welfare Mom is on the rolls an average of 14 months. Nationally, 65 percent are off welfare in less than two years.

The government has cracked down on welfare fraud. Independent studies place fraud and overpayment errors at about 5 percent. Still, too much, but not huge.

As for welfare recipients being mostly immigrants and minorities, in Colorado those receiving aid are about the same proportions as the general population. Are they living well on the taxpayers? Nationally, the median monthly cash benefit for a mother with two children is $365 — $4,380 a year. That is less than 40 percent of the poverty level.

In Colorado, about 3.4 percent of the population receives some form of aid. Three-quarters of that 3.4 percent are children. Nationally, after five years of rising, food stamp rolls have been falling significantly for the last 10 months. The total food stamp program costs 23 billion dollars annually, a tiny fraction of a multi-trillion dollar economy. It is a small price to pay to keep children from going hungry. Senators Faircloth and Gramm should be ashamed.

August 2, 1995

⋅⊱══◉══⊰⋅

Twelve Good Men and True

The jury system has been around for a very long time. It has served us well. The history is that trial by a jury of our peers can protect the innocent and put the guilty where they can do no more harm. We have always been taught that even in the most complex of cases, the common sense of a jury of ordinary citizens can usually bring about the right verdict. Why then are so many of us losing the faith? That double murder trial in Los Angeles, whose name we have promised never to mention in print, may only be part of the reason. It isn't the first trial where the jury system has not proven up to the task.

In the late nineteenth century Lizzie Borden, a wealthy young lady in New England high society, most certainly took an ax and killed her parents. It was before the days of supermarket tabloids, or supermarkets for that matter, and television news was more than a half-century away. Even so, the newspapers of the day were not above sensationalism. Reporters came from all over the country and a dozen sketch artists kept the public informed about Miss Borden's demeanor and described the new ensemble and hat that she wore each day. Fanciful sketches of the murder scene were particularly in demand. One unknown reporter even came up with the verse that was repeated by school children all over the country. "Lizzie Borden took an ax, gave her mother 40 whacks. And then when Lizzie was through, she gave her father 42." In the genteel society of the day, the jury could not believe that such a refined young lady could have committed such a heinous act. The fact that she had burned her bloody clothing before it could be used in evidence or that she was the only one in the locked house with her parents did little to shake the jury's faith.

When the system fails, sometimes it convicts the innocent. The Sacco-Vanzetti Case in 1919 was probably the last time that two unquestionably innocent men were executed in the United States. A shoe factory payroll had been taken in South Braintree, Massachusetts by four men and two guards had been shot. Two Italian immigrant-anarchists, Nicola Sacco and Bartolomeo Vanzetti, had been arrested for handing out pamphlets. One of the witnesses to the robbery said that one of the robbers had a small scrub mustache. Vanzetti had a great bow-wave of a mustache, and that was enough for the South Braintree Constable.

Sixteen witnesses put Vanzetti 25 miles away from South Braintree at the time of the robbery. But it was a time in America when anarchists and immigrants were feared by many. The witnesses spoke little English and jabbering in Italian did little to impress the jury. One witness put Vanzetti at the scene, but he had originally said that he couldn't remember what any of the robbers looked like. He had been taken to see Vanzetti in his cell before the identification at the trial. Unlike Miss Borden's jury, this jury was only too ready to believe that these men could have committed the crime. In spite of nearly 50,000 demonstrators arriving before the execution, they were put to death on August 22, 1927.

Enough history. A few ancient mistakes don't condemn a system that has worked for centuries. It is the present that is causing us so much concern. Can a high-profile, media-drenched trial be conducted without degenerating into a long running soap opera? The answer is, "it depends."

First and foremost, it depends on the judge. If a judge fails to focus on the one overriding purpose of a trial, justice, the trial moves without direction and a goal. If the trial plods forward slowly enough, the jury has great difficulty focusing and tends to remember the last thing they heard. If "justice delayed is justice denied," then Judge Ito has little sense of justice. That trial in Los

Angeles has been dragging on at a leisurely pace for the last seven months. Even the jury complained that the court day should not last past two o'clock and it took Judge Ito a month to decide that maybe they were right. Then the judge allowed television cameras in the courtroom. Nearly every witness seemed to relish the national spotlight and played to the cameras. Under cross-examination, expert witnesses, gaining great publicity from the exposure, could hardly admit any mistakes while on national television. The attorneys for both sides were far from immune to the same temptation. They played out the case in court in front of the cameras and outside of the court making statements daily to a hungry press.

"Judge Ito has a tough job," you say, "he is doing as well as possible under the circumstances. How could it be done better?" We need only to point to Judge William Howard of South Carolina. Judge Howard presided over the tragic Susan Smith murder trial in South Carolina. Howard kept a tight rein on both the media and the lawyers. According to a former South Carolina prosecutor, "He demonstrated that a high-profile, media-type trial can be conducted in a fashion that guarantees justice." He was aided by a cast of professional lawyers. Early in the case, he imposed a gag order on attorneys. Leaks were rare and when something did leak, he came down hard. He ordered a reporter jailed when her paper published a confidential mental evaluation of Smith. Ito, who apparently likes the spotlight himself, considered a gag order but never imposed it. Leaks in Ito's court are common. Judge Howard quickly ordered David Smith to remove a photo of his two children from his lapel before he testified. Judge Ito took seven hours to decide whether prosecutor Marcia Clark could wear an angel pin on her lapel in court.

Most importantly, Judge Howard ordered no television cameras in the courtroom. In such a high profile case, he had no use for jurors who were there for book deals or long-winded lawyers or publicity-seeking witnesses. Cameras are not always wrong in court — after all, the public has a right to know — but if the goal of the trial is justice and it is so high-profile that coverage will interfere with that goal, they should be banned.

Judge Howard has reminded us that our legal system can work well and that that trial in California is an aberration. We hope other judges learn from him.

August 9, 1995

✦✦✦

Remembering Why We Liked Ike

With all the presidential hopefuls gathering as much newspaper ink and sound bites as they can accumulate, we might think the election was this November instead of next year. With the television ratings dropping on the O. J. trial, the start of football season filling the sports pages, and no one waiting in line to buy Windows 95, news editors need a new story to overwork. They have jumped on the Republican dilemma of choosing a candidate. They have a wide variety of announced candidates working very hard for the nomination and raising the substantial funds necessary for the election. We hate to burst their bubble, but they may be fighting for third prize.

Before we get to the Republican problem, we need to go back to 1946 and Ike. General Dwight David Eisenhower was America's first five-star general. They created the rank for him since the British and Germans had Field Marshals, which outranked ordinary generals and, after all, Ike was in charge. He was supreme commander of the greatest army in history and defeated the Nazis, ending the war in Europe. A dedicated and modest military man, he had little political ambition. Up until the time he announced that he was running for President in 1952, no one knew whether he was a Republican or a Democrat. But that was later.

In 1946, Ike had dinner in Tokyo with General Douglas MacArthur. MacArthur predicted that one or the other of them would be President. Ike didn't like the publicity-seeking, pompous MacArthur and was annoyed by the suggestion that he had a hidden political agenda. He lectured MacArthur on the separation of the military from civilian politics and his own desire to run for office. When it was over, MacArthur patted him on the knee and said, "That's all right, Ike. You go on like that and you'll get it for sure."

Ike went on to be the first commander of NATO and stayed out of politics until 1952. It turned out, although it was not public knowledge at the time, that Ike was a Republican. He had voted Republican in 1932, 1936 and 1940. But he had strong ideas about America's role in the world and did not want to turn the country over to the Republican isolationists of the time.

With Truman not running in the 1952 elections, the Korean War dragging on, and the Democrats having been in the White House since 1933, a Republican victory seemed assured. Ike was concerned that MacArthur might get the nomination — a man that he said was "now as always, an opportunist." Worse, Robert Taft was the frontrunner. Ike said of him, "A very stupid man . . . he has no intellectual ability, nor any comprehension of the issues of the world." The warrior resigned his command, came home to Abilene, Kansas in June 1952 and won a bitterly contested nomination from Robert Taft. Running to keep someone else out of office is not unique. John F. Kennedy said during the 1960 campaign, "I have an awesome responsibility. I am the only man that stands between Nixon and the White House."

In 1953, Eisenhower became the thirty-fourth President of the United States and was reelected in 1956. He never satisfied the conservatives of his party or the liberals of the opposition, but he presided over a remarkable period of peace and prosperity in America.

Back to the present and another general on the horizon and the Republicans fighting over third place. General Colin Powell is being touted as the next President. Polls last week showed him winning a three-way race with President Clinton and Senator Dole.

Who is this Colin Powell? The son of Jamaican immigrants in Harlem, he went to public schools and joined ROTC at the City College of New York. He served two tours in Viet Nam. After serving as Ronald Reagan's National Security Advisor, Powell rejoined the Army in 1989. But within a year George Bush promoted him to become, at 52, the youngest ever Chairman of the Joint Chiefs of Staff, the position from which he directed the Gulf War. The war's stunning success earned him enough accolades for a lifetime. Is he a Republican? Is he a

Democrat? Well, if there was still a center to both those parties he could be either, but neither party, living as they are in the grip of their extreme wings, could embrace [him]. He believes in personal responsibility. He is the perfect anti-victim, validating America's fondest dream that anyone with few advantages can rise to the top without bitterness and without forgetting who he is. Powell praises entrepreneurship and worries about the Democrats' tendency to embrace victimhood. Then he must be a Republican. He is against abortion, but does not believe that the government should interfere. He believes in personal responsibility without excessive welfare, but said, "not every American can lift themselves by their own bootstraps. All do not have bootstraps, some do not have boots."

Where does he fit? He fits with the vast majority of the country that is not looking at single issues or extremes. We hope that he runs. We hope that he does not run with either party. They are too far right and too far left for Powell and for America. No third-party candidate has ever won the Presidency. With the major parties on the fringes of American belief, now is the time. What we need is a fine American for President.

In the final hours of the Republican Convention of 1952, Ike's supporters started wearing "I Like Ike" buttons. Taft's supporters wore, "But what does Ike like?" buttons. It wasn't what he liked that counted. It was his integrity and ability that got him elected.

September 20, 1995

⋆⇒◯⇐⋆

It Hasn't Changed All that Much

We went to the community benefit for the Norwood-Redvale Volunteer Fire Department last week and it gave us new insights into national politics. That may seem a bit farfetched, but we'll explain in a minute. First, a little about the benefit.

Like the seven words you can't say on the radio, *The Post* keeps a list of words and phrases we will never print in the paper. They include such words as *prioritize* and *legitimatize* and *kudos* and *downsizing*. Among them is the phrase *sense of community*.

We didn't ban that phrase because we thought it was inherently offensive, but because of its chronic misuse. It was generally brought up at town and county government meetings in the sentence, "How can the government better maintain our *sense of community.*" We moderated quite a few forums over the years for candidates running for local office and invariably every one of the candidates was for *sense of community.* Having an innate belief that a community is made up of the individuals and families who work and struggle to keep it alive and that, at best, government can only act to support those individuals, we are skeptical of politicians using the jargon.

Well, we acquired a real sense of the Wright's Mesa community last week. An overflow crowd packed the Community Center and cheered the volunteers and put over $9,000 towards improving equipment for the department. It is enough to give even a cynical editor renewed faith in the continuing strength of rural America.

We didn't forget the new found political insight we promised to share. We had come to the auction to give some money to the Fire Department and to perhaps pick up something useful. We went through some things we didn't want and others we couldn't afford and were starting to think of just donating the money and going back to work on the paper, when we saw the item we just had to have. We ended up in a spirited bidding war and spent more than we intended, but we will never have buyer's remorse.

We bought an original Harry Truman campaign poster from the 1944 election. The poster now hangs above our desk and it gives us inspiration to compare his campaign to the current presidential year.

Truman wasn't running for president in 1944. He was Roosevelt's running mate. Vice presidents, then as now, were mostly around for show. He was a mid-westerner and a loyal party member and the party bosses felt he wouldn't be much of a threat to whichever candidate they picked to succeed Roosevelt in 1948. We wrote some time ago about how Truman described his decision to drop the bomb on Hiroshima. Truman and the office of vice president were held in such little esteem in 1944 that he was not even told of the Manhattan Project to produce the atomic bomb until after he became president.

Roosevelt was inaugurated for his third term on January 20, 1945. He died 82 days later. Truman became president.

Although Truman did a remarkable job of leading the nation through the final months of the war and the enormous adjustment to a peacetime economy, he was very unpopular. It would be difficult to believe from the newspapers of the day that future historians would consider Truman a great president. He presided over the Marshall Plan's reconstruction of Europe, the bringing of democracy to Japan and faced the Berlin blockade with remarkable strength and restraint.

He got credit for little at the time and his critics were numerous. Attacked as too liberal by the southern "dixiecrat" wing of the party and too conservative by the liberal wing, Truman was so unpopular by the time the congressional elections of 1946 rolled around [that] there was a Republican sweep. The Republicans had not controlled the White House or either House of Congress since 1932. Bob Taft, the new Senate majority leader, supported by a press far to the right of today's media, attacked Truman at every turn.

Does any of this sound familiar? Future historians can write much of the political history of 1994 to 1996 by just changing the dates from half a century earlier.

Truman's prospects didn't look any better as the 1948 nominating convention drew near. He had none of Roosevelt's charisma. He lacked the wicked grin, the tilted cigarette holder, the pince-nez glasses and the prep school accent. Truman was average in height and appearance. He had a flat, high-pitched voice and he had never learned to read a speech. His head hung over the manuscript, and he had no sense of pace or emphasis.

"Truman is a gone goose," said Republican Congresswoman Claire Booth Luce, and no Democrats contradicted her. Convinced that Truman couldn't win, the Democrats courted Dwight Eisenhower. Some say that even Truman wanted Eisenhower to run in his place, although Truman never mentions it in his memoirs. Of course, they couldn't get Eisenhower. In stark contrast to MacArthur, during his entire military career

Eisenhower kept to his principle that the military should never speak out on domestic politics. The Democrats didn't know that Ike had always voted Republican. They would find out four years later. When Eisenhower turned down the Democrats unequivocally a month before the convention, Boss Hague reportedly crunched out his cigar, saying, "Truman, Harry Truman. Oh my God!" "The Democrats act as though they have accepted an invitation to a funeral," the *Associated Press* reported on the eve of the convention.

The Republicans nominated Thomas Dewey, Governor of New York. He chose the popular Governor of California and future Chief Justice, Earl Warren, as his running mate. Dewey spoke of national unity as his theme. "Our people yearn to higher ground to find common purpose in the finer things which unite us . . . ," said Dewey in his acceptance speech. It would have made a great television spot today. The Democrats started thinking about 1952 as their next hope, and Mrs. Dewey started thinking about redecorating the White House, and Bob Taft started thinking about repealing all the legislation of the Roosevelt era.

The Gallop Poll gave Dewey a 20-point lead. *Newsweek* magazine carried the cover headline, "Fifty Political Experts Unanimously Predict a Dewey Victory." Maybe experts haven't changed all that much in half-a-century. Newspapers haven't either.

The *Chicago Tribune* had always hated Harry Truman, just as they had always hated Roosevelt, calling for his impeachment on several occasions. But here they were at 7:45 p.m. election night, the printing deadline for the morning's first edition, without a clear trend in the voting. The editor needed a headline. He couldn't just say that there was an election yesterday. The first returns were in from New England, but they generally reflected city votes that were predominantly Democrat strongholds. Truman was leading, but the editor knew what everyone knew: Dewey would win. The infallible Gallop Poll was still predicting a Dewey landslide. The editor had a five-column bold headline set in type. "Dewey Defeats Truman."

They were wrong of course.

It was a Truman landslide, 304 electoral votes to 189. The Democrats swept Congress as well. When the triumphant President returned to Washington holding aloft the *Chicago Tribune's* proclamation of his defeat, he was greeted by a cheering crowd of 750,000 people. On the *Washington Post* newspaper building was a huge banner, "Mr. President, we are ready to eat crow whenever you are ready to serve it."

How could everyone have been so wrong?

Time magazine wrote in November 1948, " . . . the press had delegated its journalist's job to the polls." As we said, things haven't changed all that much in 50 years.

May 29, 1996

Not with a Bang, but a Whimper

If everyone likes what you say, it is not news. It is show business. The same can be said for politics. Democracy by its very nature is messy and spontaneous. When it is carefully scripted and when all the outcomes have been pre-decided, it is much less messy, but it isn't democracy. It is also deadly dull. Despite extensive news coverage of the Republican Convention and the huge pre-Democratic Convention media blitz this weekend, the country has reacted with a rousing ho-hum and given the conventions the lowest TV ratings since ratings have been kept.

Is this just another example of political apathy in '90s America? I don't think so. There is nothing going on at the conventions. All of the decisions have been made and only the show business remains.

In order to generate interest in the Democratic Convention, television news has bombarded us with images of the confrontations of the 1968 convention. It is interesting to watch the 1996 Dan Rather commenting on the 1968 Dan Rather being roughed up on the convention floor by Mayor Daley's thugs. It is disturbing to watch the confrontations between the Chicago police and the protesters outside the convention hall.

In contrast, this year's Republican Convention was a love fest. Carefully scripted, the uninformed would have thought from the parade of minority speakers and pro-choice delegates that the Republicans were the party of affirmative action and choice. Elizabeth Dole's virtuoso performance on the convention floor raised her husband's poll percentages by ten points, as if the speaking ability of the candidate's wife is a deciding issue. Lest you think this is a Republican ploy, I predict that Clinton will have his own parade of military and police uniforms as he tries to cast the Democrats as the party of military power and law and order. Surely the media will make endless comparisons between Elizabeth Dole's performance and Hillary Clinton's upcoming time on stage. Will that help you pick your candidate?

Will there be inspiring speeches from the candidates, giving insight into their future performance in office? The speeches will be inspiring, attesting to the abilities of the best speechwriters that money can buy. They will give insight into how the candidates' handlers are reading the polls, but will tell us little of the candidates themselves.

It wasn't always this way. Before the primary system gave the nomination to the candidate with the most campaign funding, the most stamina and the most special interest zealots, the conventions actually picked the candidates. The troubles of the historic 1968 convention say more about America in 1968 than they do about political conventions. We have to travel back to the Democratic Convention of 1912 to see how representative government can work in this republic.

It was a steam bath of heat and humidity, marking the worst of Atlantic Coast summers that greeted the delegates to Baltimore in late June of 1912. Democratic Presidential hopefuls were much in evidence. There was Ohio's Governor Judson Harmon, the choice of most staunch conservatives. There was Indiana's bland but amiable Governor Thomas R. Marshall. There was the South's favorite son, Oscar W. Underwood, Congressman from Alabama. Most important, there was Missouri's Champ Clark, Speaker of the House, old-time liberal and the choice of William Randolph Hearst. Clark was a ringing orator, who had delivered hundreds of speeches at county fairs around the nation. The Clark organization rolled into Baltimore on the old B&O Railroad with 324 delegates, an army of supporters and a theme song. They marched down Charles Street shouting the song that was their Missouri man's theme,

"I don't care if he is a houn',
You gotta quit kickin' my dawg aroun'."

Fortunately his main competition was not there to hear it. Woodrow Wilson, first-term Governor of New Jersey, college professor and former president of Princeton, had chosen to go to the governor's summer cottage at Sea Girt, New Jersey, to sit out the convention.

Dedicated suffragist Mrs. Mary Arkwright Hutton of Spokane, Washington was one of only two women delegates in 1912. In her trademark scarlet suit and sweeping straw hat, she was much sought out by reporters. She said of Wilson, "No man who has been a schoolmaster all his life is quite big enough to be President of the United States." Many agreed with her. But there was that night in Trenton in 1910 when New Jersey Party Boss Big Jim Smith had put him over the top as Democratic candidate for governor. Smith thought Wilson would be a puppet for the party machine. He learned differently from Wilson's acceptance speech moments later. Wilson accepted the nomination with a ringing declaration of independence. Reformers who had bitterly fought him an hour before listened in astonishment. Long after Wilson had finished his speech, they stood on their seats and in the aisles crying, "Go on! Go on!" What speechwriter today could have found the soul of the candidate as Wilson did on his own?

Could Wilson possibly win the Presidential nomination? He had antagonized the party bosses with his independence as governor. Clark had the Hearst papers behind him and Tammany Boss Charlie Murphy. The Cook County Democratic Club of Chicago arrived behind a fifty-piece band supporting Clark.

Wilson had his supporters as well — Princeton students shouting for him and his trusted advisors. Wilson had less than a third of the delegates. His staunchest supporter was William Gibbs McAdoo, the builder of the Hudson Tubes, who coined the Progressive [Party] slogan, "The public be pleased." McAdoo arrived at Wilson headquarters to find his campaign in shambles. All appeared lost.

On the afternoon of June 23, a balding, pale old man in a crumpled alpaca coat arrived at Baltimore's Union Station. William Jennings Bryan, three times Democratic candidate and shopworn standard-bearer, would change the course of American history at that convention. Angered that Tammany Hall and other Easterners who led the party to ruin in 1904 were again trying to gain control, he rallied the Progressives to stop them. He cajoled, convinced and organized, and in the end he supported Wilson.

There were fifteen-thousand delegates and spectators packing the sweltering convention hall. Speakers depended on megaphones and lung capacity to sway the crowd. Attention spans were short, awaiting the invention of air conditioning a generation later. It took 768 votes to nominate. After ten ballots, the count was Clark-556, Wilson-350. After fourteen ballots Clark had gained seven more votes and was calling for Wilson's capitulation.

Bryan jumped on his chair, waved his palm leaf fan and demanded the right to explain his vote. He was hopelessly out of order. It did not stop him. In the same rich baritone that delivered the "Cross of Gold" speech 18 years before, he began, "I cast my vote for Governor Wilson." He turned the tide. During the next ten ballots, 100,000 telegrams arrived at convention headquarters supporting Wilson. It took another week and a total of 46 ballots, but Wilson would receive the nomination.

I thought I might watch the Democratic Convention on television this week if I need some sleep. If I want to stay awake, I have a book on Teddy Roosevelt's nomination at the Progressive Party Convention that can provide far more excitement than anything Campaign '96 has to offer.

August 28, 1996

-→-≡◯⊂=-→-

JAPANESE ATTACKED 53 YEARS AGO TODAY

PEARL HARBOR BOMBED

The Roosevelt's had 30 guests for lunch in the Blue Room of the White House a little after noon on December 7, 1941. The Washington Redskins were playing their last football game of the season against the Philadelphia Eagles in the ancient Griffith Stadium. J. Edgar Hoover had taken the weekend off to go to New York.

The chief radioman for the U.S. Navy's Washington communication station, Frank A. Ackerson, was called on the Hawaii frequency and asked to stand by for an urgent message: "AIR RAID PEARL HARBOR. THIS IS NO DRILL." There were few details. The message was passed up the line to Frank Knox, Secretary of the Navy. He responded, "Those little yellow bastards!" Political correctness hadn't been invented yet. He passed the message to Roosevelt.

Although Roosevelt was profound on many occasions and eminently quotable, he is reported to have said only one word on learning of the attack, "No!"

Hoover's chief agent in Honolulu called him in New York. "You can hear the bombs yourself!" He held the phone out the window for Hoover to hear.

Although the media of the time minimized the losses, the damage was enormous. Nineteen ships including seven battleships were sunk or seriously damaged and 3,000 Americans lost their lives. On December 8, a Declaration of War against Japan was passed by Congress. The sole dissenting vote was cast by Rep. Jeannette Rankin, Republican of Montana. She had also cast the sole dissenting vote against entering World War I. On December 10, the Japanese invaded Luzon in the Philippines. On December 11, Germany and Italy declared war against the United States. On December 22, Wake Island fell to the Japanese after a heroic 15-day stand by 400 U.S. Marines.

From January to May of 1942, the Japanese had it all their way. Manila fell, Bataan fell, Corregidor fell and the Navy suffered additional heavy losses to Japan in the Battle of the Java Sea. But exceptional skill and courage on the part of U.S. forces started to change things even in those early dark days. Major General James H. Doolittle struck the first offensive blow in the Pacific by raiding Tokyo with carrier-launched bombers. The raid was significant in the consternation it caused in Japan and its boost to American morale. 1942 was the year that the United States started on the long road to victory.

By summer, the United States scored naval victories in the Coral Sea and at Midway and the Marines landed on Guadalcanal. By November in the European theater, U.S. forces began landing in North Africa. Lt. General Dwight Eisenhower commanded 50 vessels and 400,000 troops in a prelude to his command of the largest invasion force ever to be assembled. This was only two years before Normandy.

On August 15, 1945, less than four years after Japan's sneak attack on Pearl Harbor, their unconditional surrender was signed aboard the U.S.S. Missouri in Tokyo Bay. Many brave Americans lost their lives in the conflict. We owe them a lasting debt of gratitude.

December 7, 1994

From the Front Page of the Daily Planet, *May 6, 1994: Peter Spencer and Roudy Roudebush, a couple of ink-stained wretches, delivered Spencer's entry intro the area's newspaper field Wednesday, with the* Norwood Post.
Photo courtesy of the *Daily Planet* and Doug Berry, enhanced by Steve Larson

CHAPTER SIX

A View from the Canyon ... Wayward Politics and the Environment

Preliminaries . . .

When Peter Spencer moved to Telluride in 1979, the place was wild and raucous — as a fledgling ski resort town should be. The newcomers, who came from far and wide, spent a good deal of time getting acquainted in the social hubs of the community — the bars. Personal tales from pre-Telluride days, along with the sagas of local politics, were swapped with great flair, colored by the consumption of fermented beverages and clouds of cigarette smoke. In this milieu of new beginnings and high times, I met Peter. His station of choice was the barstool next to the door at the New Sheridan Bar, a haunt favored by the likes of Roudy Roudebush, Ed Bowers and George Greenbank. And on many a night, above the clinking of glasses, the telling of good stories and an equal number of bad jokes, could be heard a distinct and heartfelt laugh. It is what I first remember about Peter Spencer.

At the time, I was a young writer, wanna-be ski bum and tundra-hugger fresh from Alaska. Peter was a street-savvy industrialist from New York City who could, and often did, talk circles around the discords of my youthful idealism. We hit it off instantly. Neither of us let our divergent beliefs or our dissimilar backgrounds get in the way of a good yarn or our mutual respect for one another. I watched, as the ever-accessible Peter, like a duck drawn to water, became more and more involved in Telluride's divisive and often litigious politics. No sooner elected to town council, Peter was appointed mayor. He was an articulate and powerful persuader; his ability to give credence to his adversaries' positions, even if he didn't agree with them, won him immediate and lasting respect.

In 1991, Peter went to work for Telluride Publishing, the magazine-producing company I was employed by. He was hired to usher the company into the computer age. I dug in my heels. I was no fan of technology. I would have written the magazine by hand if I thought anyone would read it. I was good at cut-and-paste; it was a mindless, rather Zen task, that got me away from the phone. Nonetheless, Peter installed a little Apple computer — one-tenth the size of our old Compugraphic typesetter — and patiently proceeded to cajole me into a healthy relationship with the alien machine. Soon, I had no idea how we had put out a magazine without a computer, or Peter Spencer.

When Peter told me he wanted to start his own newspaper in Norwood, I tried my damnedest to discourage him. I had newspaper experience of my own and knew the commitment it took to run a small town weekly. It was worse than a restaurant. It was a marriage with no honeymoon, with no time off, the publisher more vulnerable than a politician. But Peter was ready to write. All those stories, ideas and reflections needed a venue. And Peter Spencer knew how to write.

Peter put poetry in prose (he loved Longfellow). He could color the dullest topic and flavor it with salt and sage. He often called or stopped by the magazine office to run his upcoming op-ed past his old — but younger — colleagues. I often just shook my head, especially if he was proposing some rant against coyotes or environmentalists. I asked him to write a few history articles for the magazine, which he accomplished with a wit and wisdom as only he could. Not surprisingly, reader surveys showed that the history pieces were the favorite topic in the publication.

I still send Peter an email every now and then. He was such a computer geek, I am sure he still receives them. One day, I expect a witty and wise voice reply — delivered by Mac-programmed software, of course — followed by a big hearty laugh.

I keep checking.

Mary Duffy

Damming the Upper San Miguel to Protect It, an Idea Worthy of the Queen of Hearts. Who Speaks for the Trout?

There was a military strategy that was in vogue some years ago: destroy villages to prevent them from falling into the hands of the enemy. Since falling into the hands of the enemy was considered a fate worse than death, blow the place up and you win. Since no villagers could be interviewed later to confirm that preference, the policy continued for some time. I haven't thought about destroying things to save them for quite some time, that is, until reports from the Telluride Council last Wednesday discussing the good guys building a dam to save the river from the bad guys.

It is a bad idea. It always was a bad idea, and it will continue to be a bad idea. It is fostered by a long series of theories, based on good intentions, but grounded in a nonexistent fact base. The San Miguel is one of the last un-dammed tributaries of the Colorado. To endorse a dam on that river based on misinformation in unconscionable.

First, let us examine the famous 6.5 cfs minimum stream flow. When the Town of Telluride and the Mountain Village first started negotiating about water in the river, no one knew what the stream flow was in the San Miguel running through Telluride. The town's consulting engineer did some preliminary studies on the river running through town and determined that the river flowed as low as 8 or 9 cfs during the December through February period of 1981. That low flow was not caused by anyone taking water out of the river; it is caused by the fact that it is all the water that is in the river at its upper end at some times of the year. It was usually above 12 cfs during that time, but on very cold days the flow got as low as 8 cfs. Flow measurements are not precise unless you run the whole river through a pipe so you know exact volume. You put a propeller in the river, gauge the speed and then interpolate the flow based on your estimated cross section of the river at the point of measurement. This is why the ditch companies use headgates to insure fairness and accuracy. In any event, when the water level was interpolated to be 8 cfs at Mahoney Drive, you could walk on the rocks across the river. This indicates that 6.5 cfs is pretty low. The rest of the year, the San Miguel usually flows at considerably higher rates through the town.

At Society Turn, the river flows at considerably higher rates all the time, because there are additional tributaries feeding the river, and by the time you get past Ilium, the flows are usually adequate to maintain the ecology of the river. So, the problem only exists on the river through the Town of Telluride, not lower down on the river, and it only exists in the low flow winter months. It would be nice to maintain a flow of 12 to 15 cfs in the river in those low flow months. The hydro plant will not accomplish that end under any circumstance. As a legal maneuver, the construction of the hydro plant might prevent someone from taking water out of the river at certain times, but it doesn't put any water into the river; it only dams it and it will dry up its own section of the river in the process. For the length of the hydro plant's penstock, there will not be 12 cfs or 6.5 cfs, there will be zero cfs. Is this a way to save the river?

This might not work, but give it a try. Telski and the Mountain Village have plenty of water rights. What they don't have is storage. They can't effectively spread their snowmaking over six months. The Town of Telluride has storage, fifteen-hundred acre feet in Blue Lake. When does Telski need water? In October, November and early December to make snow. The town, Telski and the Metro District could make an agreement using Metro District water rights and town storage for the town to release water from its storage to augment the water flows in the river at the times of highest demand and lowest to keep the stream flow at a reasonable level. Yes, it would be a tough agreement to make, but it sure beats damming the river.

Speaking of legal maneuvers, the town has criminalized excessive water use and has passed the first reading of an ordinance placing a whole new layer of regulation and enforcement on what kind of grass to plant and when to water. It is a step, but wouldn't charging for water used be the logical way to approach the problem? (With flat rate charges, as are in use in Telluride, the more water you use, the cheaper it is per gallon.)

A government that charges less per gallon of water for higher usage is in no position to judge what's best for the river. Use charges work in almost every water system in America, why not in Telluride?

As for the hydro plant saving oil or coal or global warming, the only time you save generating capacity is when you reduce peak demand, thereby taking fossil fuel plants off line, or when you can generate hydro to offset peak demand. The peak demand for power in the Telluride region is during those same months that the river's flow is at its lowest. The hydro plant would be barely producing any power at all during those months because of insufficient flow in the river.

If it costs the town $300,000 to not be responsible for putting the first dam on the San Miguel, it's worth every cent.

August 17, 1994

⟡

Just the Facts Ma'am, Just the Facts

Baxter Black described an environmentalist in a recent column as someone that believed in global cooling 20 years ago and believes in global warming today. That's probably a little harsh; after all you can't predict the weather, but there is some truth in the assertion. Basic science is a complex subject and new reports of the basic research attempt to summarize data that is not readily summarized. Scanning less than perfect summaries of less than complete studies generally leads to taking courses of action that are both unnecessary and ineffective. After all [that] oat bran that everyone was eating to stay healthy, additional research indicates that oat bran was not better for anyone than any other bran.

Fad diets are not nearly as serious as long-range weather forecasting. When the weather bureau talks about a long-range forecast, they are talking about seven days. When they go way out on a limb, it is one month. Why then are so many non-climatologists so dead certain that there will be serious global warming over the next ten to fifty years? And why are they equally certain that the warming will be a disaster? A recent Yale study of worldwide food production indicates that food supply would be increased by global warming. Combine that with a joint British/American study that indicates that increased particulate matter in the atmosphere is making clouds more reflective, leading to a hypothesis that the global cooling that more reflective clouds will create, will more than offset the warming effect of greenhouse gases.

Where does that leave us? I looked at our satellite picture on the next page and I don't think that it is going to rain this week. I wonder if there is Global Drying.

August 24, 1994

-⊷⇒◠⊶-

If You Think It's Crowded, Just Wait

There was a lot to do in *Norwood Post* Country this Labor Day Weekend. There was a reunion of the old Bedrock school in Paradox; there was a reunion of the residents and miners of Uravan; there was Calamity Town outside of Naturita, the Rodeo in Ridgway, the Film Festival in Telluride, the Elk Ranch tour in Norwood, and the chili cook-off at the Hitchin' Post.

We spent a lot of time driving around *Post* Country taking pictures and talking to people. There was one constant this weekend. There were people everywhere.

Now, the western part of our area is one of the least densely populated places in America. San Miguel County, as a whole, has 1,286 square miles and 3,653 people. That is a population density of 2.8 people per square mile. The Census Bureau considers any county with less than 3 people per square mile a "frontier county," whatever that may be. In the area of the county including

Placerville, east to Telluride and on to Ophir, there are 2,455 people and 357 square miles. That is a density of 6.9 per square mile. The rest of the county, Norwood and the West End has 1,198 and 929 square miles. That is 1.3 people per square mile. The western end of Montrose County has 1,109 square miles and 2,289 people for a density of 2.1 people per square mile.

Now, if you are not familiar with census density figures, it might sound like less than 3 people per square mile is a decent number. What with the mountains and dry mesas being largely uninhabitable, one might consider that enough. Consider, however, that in 1790, when the first official U.S. census was taken, there were 4.5 people per square mile in the original 13 colonies. That's nearly twice the density that we have in our corner of Colorado over 200 years later. We may not have caught up to the 1790 figures yet, but the rest of the country is off and running. In 1990, the nearly 4 million square miles of the United States were home to 248 million people. That is a density of 70 people per square mile. If current population trends continue, there will be nearly 400 million people in the U.S. in 2050, and that is more than 100 per square mile. That projection is based on current birth and death and immigration rates.

If you think 100 people per square mile is way too many, there is Bangladesh. They have 2,365 people per square mile. That would be the equivalent of having 3,000,000 people in San Miguel County. That's a lot of water taps. That was last year. It should top 3,000 people per square mile by 1999. Their birth rate is three times ours.

There is a U.N. sponsored world population conference in Cairo this week. Cairo has a population density that is ten times that of New York City. The conference has been wracked with controversy over abortion, national sovereignty, women's rights, religion and hundreds of competing special agendas. But the essential goal of the conference, the reduction in the rate of growth of the world's population, is probably the single most important goal in maintaining a world with the resources and room for our children's children, and the birds and the trees and the rest of the world as we know it.

I don't have any suggestions for the population conference. There is no easy solution, maybe the world has to get past the details and go to work on the goal.

Three years ago at the Opera House in Telluride, I was the moderator of a conference on the increased pressures of so-called industrial tourism on the environment. Most of the panel discussed things like how many ski areas shouldn't be built or whether you should throw trout back or eat them. There were discussions of mountain bikes versus backpackers versus four-wheelers. There used to be room for all of them, but now it seemed as if each group wanted to limit the other group's use of what open space is left so their group could use the space for their higher purpose.

One of the members of the panel was David Brower. He was an early president of the Sierra Club and is considered by many an elder statesman of the environmental movement. I fully expected him to talk about open space or predators or trees. I was wrong. He didn't say anything for most of the discussion, and I wondered if his advanced years had muted his once eloquent voice. I was wrong. After everyone else had finished with their plan for saving the environment for people just like themselves, Brower spoke. His voice filled the Opera House. I wrote down every word.

"While you have bickered over details, the population of the world has grown. It is growing at an unsupportable rate as I speak these words. There is no way to save the environment that supports man's life on earth if there are ten billion people. There are more people alive today than have lived in all of human history. In less than twenty years that population will double again. Do not argue over the details of short-term measures. Act now."

Now there's an environmental message that makes sense.

September 7, 1994

⤏⟶◉⟵⤎

Forests and Grasslands

Several months ago we wrote about global warming. We wrote that there has been scant evidence that it has occurred and that the mathematical models that predicted an environmental warming disaster over the next half century have been demonstrated to have serious flaws. Short-term weather forecasting leaves much to chance; long-term climate forecasting hasn't reached the status of serious science yet.

Not content to let other favorite theories stand on their laurels, we decided to look at forests and their relationship to the global warming theory. For a long time now, we have been told that forests trap carbon dioxide and keep it out of the atmosphere and that logging and grazing destroy the forests and therefore contribute to higher carbon dioxide in the atmosphere. This theory is part of the philosophical foundation of the movement to seriously restrict logging and grazing in the West, and especially in *Norwood Post* Country. Of course, irresponsible logging and careless overgrazing should be strongly discouraged, but is all logging and grazing a problem for the environment? The answer may be quite the opposite.

T. R. Seastedt, a University of Colorado biologist, reports that "grazing opens the canopy, maintains the foliage in a young physiological state, improves photosynthesis and increases nitrogen availability to plant roots. Temperate grasslands are superior soil carbon sinks when compared to forests. Forests release their carbon storage during and after wildfires, where carbon stored by grass stays in the root system." Since increased carbon dioxide in the atmosphere accelerates grass growth, the storage system itself is self-regulating.

Seastedt doesn't have all the answers. Based on his studies, we wouldn't presume to suggest cutting all the forests for lumber and then planting grass for grazing in order to save the world from global warming. But then again, we never believed in global warming in the first place.

December 7, 1994

-◦▸══◉══◂◦-

I'll Huff and I'll Puff and I'll Blow Your Condo Down

Back in the Fourteenth Century, according to historian Barbara Tuckman, after childbirth and the plague, it is likely that the leading cause of death among children in Europe was being eaten by wolves. The fear of going into the woods, the trials and tribulations of Little Red Riding Hood (who was, by the way, saved by a logger), the legends of the werewolves, and the cautionary tale of the three pigs probably all stem from ancient fears of these most efficient of predators. There is another side to the wolf legends. There was the story of Romulus and Remus, suckled by wolves before they grew up to found the Roman Empire. The wolf spirit is a strong, positive force in the legends of the Native Americans of the Rocky Mountains. And after all, Kevin Costner danced with a wolf on the big screen. It was inevitable that the issue of wolf reintroduction would raise passion on both sides.

In the 1920s, the federal government initiated a program to eradicate wolves from Yellowstone Park and the Rocky Mountain states. The program was successful. Now the federal government is spending 12.8 million dollars to reintroduce 29 wolves of the subspecies *canus lupus irremotis* from Canada into Yellowstone. Michael Robinson, the director of Sinapu, a wolf support group in Boulder, says that this is a first step and that Sinapu hopes to introduce wolves to Colorado in the next five years. He said, "The San Juans, of course, are probably the wildest part of Colorado, and hold the most potential for bringing wolves back to Colorado." We always thought Boulder was the wildest part of Colorado, but we'll take his word for it. He said that "all we are talking about is restoring natural conditions." We suppose he means natural conditions here in the San Juans; we don't think he's talking about rototilling the jogging paths in Boulder.

We've given some thought as to what "natural conditions" are, and whether they should be restored. To aid us in this quest, we studied up on the history of northwestern Wyoming and Montana. Yellowstone Park was created in 1872. It had been a hunting ground for Paleo-Indians since the end of the last Ice Age, when they hunted the wooly mammoth to extinction. The Paleo-Indians were somewhat higher on the food chain than the wolves.

In more recent times the area was a hunting ground for the Crow tribes. A treaty in 1868 gave the Crow hunting rights in most of Yellowstone. Four years later, in typical federal fashion, the government reneged on the treaty and kicked the Crow out.

The Crow were pretty efficient predators. They kept the elk numbers down and there was little game for competing species. Therefore, there were virtually no wolves in the park in 1872. With the Crow, or for that matter anyone else, no longer allowed to hunt Yellowstone, the elk and deer populations burgeoned, largely at the expense of the vegetation. The wolves, no longer having to compete with the Crow, also made a comeback. By 1920, wolves were everywhere, and outside the park, the wolves were finding easy prey among the sheep and cattle. They could return to the park for sanctuary after their nightly forays. Ranching losses to predators were huge. The federal government, who, even then, never saw a problem that wasn't theirs to solve, eradicated the wolves. As with most federal programs, the law of unintended consequences was in full operation. In the years since the wolf eradication, the deer and elk populations, protected from all predators (even the bears are thoughtfully being fed by the tourists), have wiped out much rare vegetation and have significantly reduced the numbers of non-game animals.

If we want to return the park to "natural conditions," which date should we choose as our baseline? Sinapu seems to be aiming for somewhere between 1900 and 1920. By that time, Yellowstone had a great hotel and lots of amenities. Hardly "natural conditions". There are other choices. It doesn't seem likely that we can return to the end of the last Ice Age, both the Paleo-Indians and the woolly mammoths are gone. We suggest that we return Yellowstone to its natural condition of 1869. It was far more natural than 1920. You can't do that without significantly reducing the elk and deer populations. Wolves aren't the answer, Native Americans are. Let's honor the 1868 treaty with the Crow and let them hunt the Yellowstone. We'd be living up to our commitments and undoing a federal mess.

The Crow solution would be a whole lot cheaper than the wolf solution. If you divide the 12.8 million dollars allocated to the wolf program by the 29 wolves, you get 445 thousand dollars per wolf. That is enough to buy each and every wolf a condo in Telluride. They'd hardly be noticed there on Friday night. Interior Secretary Babbitt hopes that the wolf population in Yellowstone will grow to 300 in the next 7 years of the program.

That would be only 42 thousand dollars a wolf and they would probably have to settle for a condo in Boulder.

By the way, about 60 wolves have migrated down from Canada into Montana. They should make it to Yellowstone on their own in the next decade, even without a federal subsidy. It seems a more "natural condition" than flying them in at taxpayer expense.

February 1, 1995

⋅→⇒◑⇐←⋅

Critter Quotas, Bad Science and Environmental Victory

We came across a fascinating piece of legal maneuvering several months ago, but found it too fantastic to write seriously about. It seems that since the Endangered Species Act was passed in the early '70s, about 50 species per year have been added to the list. Of course, we know that adding an animal to the list can cause great economic upheaval. The snail darter, which may or may not be endangered, has stopped mighty dams and the northern spotted owl, which may or may not be a separate species, has brought the unemployment level in Oregon to record highs and inflated housing costs nationally. Given these consequences, one would hope that the Interior Department, charged with adding species to the list, would be extremely careful before adding a new species. Even if the cost of protecting a species is not a consideration, an evaluation of endangerment, a careful determination that we are dealing with a separate species and an even more careful determination of what measures need to be taken for protection, should all be undertaken before any action is proposed or executed. We naively believed that it worked that way. It doesn't.

It seems that one Jasper Carlton, a conservationist from Boulder, Colorado, became frustrated with how long it took to get an animal on the endangered species list. Even though the average of 50 per year hadn't changed since Jimmy Carter was President, Mr. Carlton filed 90 lawsuits against the Fish and Wildlife Service during the Reagan Administration. He was joined in the suits by "friends of the court," including the Fund for Animals. The court cases continued through the end of the Reagan Administration and on into the Bush Administration. After President Bush lost the election, and before President Clinton took office, the government decided to settle the lawsuits, which now involved some 30 environmental groups. The settlement required the Fish and Wildlife Service to add 100 new species to the endangered list each year for four years. The *Wall Street Journal* referred to this settlement as the "Critter Quota." I refer to it as bizarre. In the rush to meet the quota, mistakes are being made. The legal settlement is taking precedence over good science and the excesses will weaken the Endangered Species Act. Nobody wins.

However, we also have some good news about the environment. We know, environmental news is supposed to be depressing. We are supposed to point to disappearing wilderness, acid lakes, vanishing forests, green house gasses, global warming, polluted air, and worsening conditions all brought about by the carelessness of man. Well folks, it just isn't working out that way. There is good news on each of the subjects we are supposed to wring our hands about.

Designated wilderness lands in the United States have doubled since 1967. Sulfur dioxide, the main cause of acid rain, produced by coal burning power plants in the United States, has dropped by 75 percent since 1970, even though coal generated electricity has doubled. Dire predictions that 50 percent of all lakes would be acid by 1990 never materialized. Approximately 4 percent of all lakes are highly acidic, a number that has been steady since tests were first taken. A 10-year government study in the United States and Canada found "no evidence of a general or unusual decline of forests due to acid rain."

Then there are the vanishing forests. Forests in the United States reached their lowest point in the 1920s. Since then, retirement of marginal farmlands and timber company reforesting has reversed the trend. In 1850 New England was 35 percent wooded. It is now 59 percent wooded. Western Europe has considerably more forest then it did a half-century ago.

As for green house gasses, the mathematical models of the atmosphere that predicted warming from increases of atmospheric carbon dioxide have not worked out. The world hasn't gotten warmer. The tiny amount of carbon dioxide in the atmosphere (350 parts per million) may not have anything to do with global climate and increases and decreases may be within normal ranges. In a new study by the Marshall Institute, Frederick Seitz, head of the Institute and former president of the National Academy of Sciences, dismisses the chances of a major global warming as "inconsequential."

Does this mean we should declare victory in the war to protect the environment and go home? We don't think so. But it does mean that we should devote some of our energies to building a strong enough economy that we can feed and clothe and educate our children and give them a chance to feed and clothe and educate their children so that they can find the time and the resources to continue to improve the environment.

April 19, 1995

Good Regulations Make Bad Science

Our energy columnist, Dave Lankutis, has moved to Pago Pago. It was not to get away from *The Post's* weekly deadline, we hope. He faxed us an article at press time, and we will publish it next week. He plans to keep us apprised of energy issues in more tropical climes. Before leaving to join the American Samoa Power Authority, Dave was an engineer with San Miguel Power Cooperative, our rural electric supplier. Yours truly serves on the board of directors. Last year, concerned about a spate of lawsuits regarding EMF (Electromagnetic Fields), causing everything from cancer in humans to dairy cows not giving milk, the Cooperative asked Dave to investigate. Dave bought a gausmeter. It seems you measure EMF in milligauses. We spent an afternoon with Dave measuring the EMF surrounding us. We found that standing under the power line in front of our house, the milligaus reading was in single digits. It moved to double digits when we stood over a buried power line. Since the dirt over a buried line does not shield EMF and you are closer to a buried line than to an overhead line, you get more EMF from buried lines. We then went inside the house and checked the appliances. A foot from the toaster we were in the hundreds, more than ten times the dose under the power line. The television wasn't much better; remember Mom always told you not to sit too close, and the worst EMF emitter in the house was the electric hair dryer. Fortunately, we don't have enough hair to use one.

Nationally, there have been many lawsuits brought over EMF exposure and many government entities are contemplating regulations to shield or move power lines. Research has shown that electrical workers in generating stations, exposed to hundreds of times the EMF of the general population, have not developed higher cancer rates than anyone else.

After an extensive study of all the data on EMF, the American Physical Society, a respected organization of 45,000 physicists, has concluded that, "Fears of EMF are groundless. Moving and shielding power lines are a huge waste of dollars that could be used for real environmental problems." Will this conclusion stop the new regulations and more lawsuits? We don't think so.

Anyone who has ever driven an electric car will tell you that it is fun, but impractical. The range is limited, the cost is unmanageable, the speed is marginal and they are generally in the class of toys. In spite of the reality, three states are requiring electric car and light truck fleets by 1998. Until a new storage battery technology is perfected, they will not be practical. In the meantime, the required electric vehicles will be run on lead acid batteries. Unlike the Energizer bunny, they will not keep going and going. But they will add lead to the environment. We have done a pretty good job of significantly reducing lead in the environment by removing lead from gasoline and by requiring catalytic converters on cars. Last week, the Carnegie Mellon Institute released a study predicting that electric vehicles running on lead acid batteries will increase lead emissions from 6 to 60 times the amount from conventionally powered cars.

Will this new research cause these states to repeal their electric car requirements? We don't think so.

In his book, *Technological Risks,* physicist H. W. Lewis said, "What some of us fear most — poisons in our drinking water, radiation in our air, pesticides on our food — pose hardly any real risk, while some we fear least — driving a car, activities in our home, crossing a street — kill hundreds of thousands a year."

Then how do we get so many regulations that do not make any sense scientifically, and why do we spend so much correcting problems that barely exist while ignoring so many real risks? Supreme Court Justice Stephen Breyer may have come up with the answer. In his book, *Breaking the Vicious Circle,* he wrote, "The country's environmental regulatory system is in chaos because it has been designed by lawyers seeking solutions to problems that to scientists are minor or nonexistent." Right on, Justice Breyer!

May 17, 1995

Who Speaks for the Humans?

We were going to write this week about the confusing proposals for a flat tax, or the need for a new school, or why so few people listened to the State of the Union Address. We were going to give the wolf debate a rest. But after last week's column, the calls and faxes have kept our phones busy and our ears ringing. If we are going to earn our self-given title of fearless, we just have to jump in one more time.

We don't think that loving people and loving the environment are mutually exclusive.

Oh, you say, that seems pretty obvious.

We used to think so too, but we have evidence that the belief that humans have a place in the environment is falling into disrepute. We will give a few examples.

Two years ago, a California woman was jogging. A mountain lion, of which we have many in Colorado, attacked her and killed her. She was not old and sick and culled from a herd. She was just slower than the big cat and defenseless against claws and teeth. The lion was later killed by a state hunter.

The story is not remarkable except for its aftermath. The woman left two orphaned children and the mountain lion left two orphaned cubs. Local environmental groups raised $26,000 for the care of the cubs. Neighbors raised $4,000 for the care of the children.

O.K., you say, that was California. Things like that don't happen in the rest of the world.

In southwest Nepal is the Royal Chitwan National Park. With the help and urging of Western environmental groups, the Nepalese government created the park to preserve natural conditions. The park is a huge jungle that is home to elephants, rhinoceroses, tigers and all matter of wildlife. The park is totally "natural" except that it doesn't have any natives. Twenty-thousand indigenous people were expelled from the thatched huts that had been their homes for tens of centuries. For generations they had hunted in the preserve for sustenance. The army now patrols the park with authority to shoot, on sight, any natives suspected of poaching. The people may be hunted, but not the animals. The natives are not allowed to gather firewood anymore. In fact, the only people allowed into the preserve are western "eco-tourists." Most arrive in Katmandu in Nepalese Airlines' 757s. The money, labor, pollution and fuel consumption of their trip is allowed. The gathering of sticks for cooking is not.

In Kenya, there is the world renowned Amboseli Wilderness Preserve. To create the preserve, the Kenyan government drove out the Masai tribe. For uncounted centuries, the Masai had grazed their cattle, their only source of wealth, on the Amboseli. They lived in harmony with the wildlife. The proud Masai are now living in poverty on the edges of the preserve.

India has the Sundarban, a forest reserve in the West Bengal State. It is home to many Bengal tigers. The tigers are protected from poachers by the Indian army. Peasants, living at the subsistence level on the edges of the Sundarban, enter the reserve to collect honey, the primary food source for their families, from the thousands of natural beehives. The tigers are protected by the army, the peasants are not. Every year about 50 of the unarmed honey-gatherers are eaten by the tigers.

We have seen fund-raisers for the tigers and we've seen horrifying pictures of elephants killed for their tusks, but we haven't seen a rush to help the honey-gatherers or the Masai. Has the pendulum swung that far?

We suggested to the earnest people from Sinapu, the wolf reintroduction lobby, that we thought it was good to be on top of the food chain. It allowed our children to walk to school and to play in the fields. We suggested that an additional big, protected predator in this county would help turn more of our remaining ranches into housing developments.

They told us that no healthy wolf had attacked a human in 500 years. A healthy, reintroduced wolf crushed the hand of a worker in Idaho last week. They told us that only wolf hybrids attacked people. We spoke to our local expert Veterinarian. He confirmed our suspicion by saying that "if they aren't hybrids when they get here, they will be in a year or two." They told us that the wolves would be good for the deer populations. When the wolves were in this county, the deer were gone. When the wolves were gone, the deer came back. When we suggested that our children would be safer if we didn't have wolves in our neighborhood, they said we had nothing to worry about. They didn't suggest them in their neighborhood, however.

Is it fair to the wolves? With the population, the roads, the cars, the livestock, the tourists, the mountain bikers, would the wolves be happy here? We think not. They belong in the nearly unpopulated areas of Western Canada and Alaska and some parts of Montana. There they can be protected and people can be protected as well.

January 31, 1996

Teach your children well. A tender and thoughtful moment between father and daughter, Meghan.
Photo courtesy of Judi Kiernan, enhanced by Tor Anderson

CHAPTER SEVEN

Teach Your Children Well . . . in the Techno-Age

Preliminaries . . .

Peter Spencer — Tinker, Tailor, Soldier, Spy — well, three out of four ain't bad (I don't think he knew how to sew). But he sure could make a computer sing and dance, especially a Macintosh.

Peter was programming computers long before most of us had a clue that a hard drive was something far more exciting than a nightmare road trip to Rico during a late spring whiteout. But once Apple invented the Mac, Peter (and I) understood that "Power to the People" was about to take on a whole new meaning. We were so excited about the new technology and its limitless business applications that we started a computer consulting company, Telluride Computer Conferences, TCC, or something like that. While we didn't make a dime (the business cards were impressive though), our friendship blossomed during those years of keeping up with the latest advancements in the industry. What I didn't teach myself about Macs, I learned from Peter, though learning from him required a great deal of patience, since he insisted on showing all the bells and whistles before he got to the nuts and bolts (he mixed his metaphors, too).

Every January during the mid- to late-80s, we religiously made the pilgrimage to San Francisco for the annual MacWorld convention, rubbing elbows (and mouse pads) with the other one-hundred thousand Mac devotees at the Moscone Center. While the tacky giveaways at each and every booth — along with the many seminars that extolled the virtues of the newest version 2.0.3-and-a-half for some new software — captured my attention, Peter prowled the convention hall in search of the latest and the most incredibly cool computer technology he could find. Upon our return home, he invariably gave an inspired and inspiring presentation to the Mac Users' Group in Telluride (MUGIT) that only remotely resembled the convention I had attended.

More importantly, it was in San Francisco where I learned from Peter that one never eats in a Chinese restaurant that doesn't display a dead duck in its storefront window, that an Ethiopian restaurant actually does offer edible food (though not eating utensils), and that no matter how sleazy the hotel, a limo will still take you there from the airport.

Peter's and my birthdays fall just three days apart (in mid-January), and often one or the other coincided with MacWorld, including my 40th and his 50th. On the latter occasion, while staying at what was our favorite hotel on Union Square, the Diva, we — Peter's wife Linda, daughter Meghan, Diane Lyons and Debbie Dinkins were along on this trip — insisted that Peter open (and admire) his 50 or so exquisitely wrapped gifts before his birthday dinner. Dinner was convened at our previously discovered favorite Chinese restaurant, The Fook. Double-entendres, replete with -overs, -ups, and -yous filled the evening's dinner conversation. And of course, there was a dead duck hanging in the front window.

From a keyboard perspective, Peter was a master at multi-tasking. Behind the wheel of an automobile . . . well, that was another matter. He was absolutely the worst driver I have ever had the misadventure to passenger with. Peter's need to constantly entertain and expound, combined with his desire to maintain eye contact with his audience were dangerous companions on Highway 1. Nonetheless, he was a computer genius, and I admired the hell out of his ability to analyze a glitch and fix it, almost effortlessly. I am not alone in cursing his absence when my computer maliciously decides to misbehave at the most inopportune moment. Yet, to tell the truth, I miss him when my computer runs perfectly.

He was unique and he was my friend. Peter Spencer: definitely NOT the same old song and dance.

Judi Kiernan

Honest, It's the Machine

Back in the days of the ancient Greek tragic theater, there was always a problem extricating the hero from the clutches of evil spirits, vengeful enemies or natural disasters. Without Arnold Shwartzenegger [sic] to come to the rescue, some of the lesser talents in the Greek playwriting world relied on the special effects of nearly three millennia ago to punish the evildoers. An Athenian, George Lucas, had invented a mechanical flying dragon of sorts. Just when you couldn't figure out how the plot was going to turn, suspended by ropes and pulleys from the top of the outdoor theater, this mechanical monster would swoop down on the stage and smite the bad guys, and save the good guys. Ancient Greeks loved to coin new names (it wasn't that hard back then, not much was named yet). They named this special effect *Deus ex Machina*, the god in the machine.

I haven't thought much about *Deus ex Machina* since I had a course in Greek theater my freshman year in college. That is, until today. I now believe that the monster is not extinct, he is alive and well and living in my computer. I didn't know he was there until he decided I was one of the bad guys and it was time to take revenge.

This story, by way of explanation, is why we don't have Tuesday night's satellite map in this week's paper.

June 8, 1994

It's only $29.95 and it Can Change Your Life

I spent a part of my life programming computers. I stopped doing it because it made conversation difficult.

"Well, what do you do for a living, Peter?"

"I write computer programs."

"Nice weather we've been having," was the usual reply. Sometimes the knowledge that I was a programmer led to questions like how to set the clock on their VCR. Usually people found a reason to freshen their drink or walk out on the porch. While we're on the subject, I've heard the statistic that 95 percent of the U.S. population can't program their VCR. It is generally quoted by someone bemoaning American technical illiteracy, or berating the school system, or saying the Japanese are going to eat our lunch. The truth of the matter is that 95 percent of the population can't program their VCR. This is not a sign of some American failure, but rather the inability of the Japanese to design a rational human interface for a VCR. When the Japanese need computer programs, they ask Microsoft or Apple or IBM. So much for longer school hours and more homework. No one can write programs in Japanese.

Back to the main subject. Sometimes I was asked what system error 18b03 meant. Fortunately, I never had any idea. The other question, which always frightened me, was, "I really need to get a computer so I can organize my life. Which kind should I get?"

At that point, I started to look for the exit or went to freshen my drink. I keep my phone numbers on rolodex and scribble my appointments on the backs of envelopes or anything else that's handy. I own a bunch of those $29.95 programs that set your schedules and call your friends and remind you to go to the dentist and keep your tax records straight. Even before I discovered the gremlins in my machine, they never did me any good. If you're basically disorganized, you're basically disorganized. I can never remember to enter the phone numbers in the computer rolodex, I forget to write lots of appointments down, and most of the time I can't remember where I put the manuals, so I don't know how to work this life-changing software anyway.

I remember those old TV commercials when you never had a date on Saturday night, or could get a job, or get your dog to wag its tail unless you bought this deodorant or that mouthwash. If you had a pimple, the world would end, but for $2.99 you could buy the cure. Remember a little dab of Brill Cream could get you a date with the homecoming queen. I always laughed at those commercials. Who could believe that their whole lives would be changed by some product that was waiting for you in the stores?

Of course, there is this new computer program. It's $39.95 and it will make me start writing my column two days earlier and will send my wife flowers on her anniversary. I just ordered it. I hope it gets here before my anniversary, which is tomorrow. It will surely change my life.

June 8, 1994

⁗⟹⟸⁗

Searching for a Scenic Overlook on the Information Highway

There is much ado about the Information Highway in the press of late. The president is for it; the vice president is for it; a whole industry of consultants has sprung up, full grown, who for a fee will explain how you can prepare for it, plan your business for it, and how it will change your life. Makes you kind of think that you might be left out in the cold if there isn't an Information Highway exit ramp on your block, and are our schools teaching our children to navigate this road or will they be doomed to menial, low paying jobs their whole lives, while Information Highway literate workers get to run the companies?

How about interactivity? Is your computer interactive? How about your TV? Will we use the Information Highway on our TV to interactively read the news? A click here, a voice command there and we can hear the speech that was quoted or see the person making the speech. Will newspapers become obsolete? Will the home-shopping network replace the Wal-Mart and will we pay our bills and research our homework through the keyboard?

The answer to all of the above questions is "NO." More on the Information Highway in a moment.

There are truly revolutionary changes in business and in day to day living that technology has brought, but the size of the change is not directly related to the complexity of the technology or the amount of money it costs. In business, the Post-It note and the fax machine have probably created more change in the last ten years than other, more highly touted technologies. The Post-It note was invented by a scientist at 3M (the people who gave us Scotch tape) when he came up with a glue that didn't stick very well and was trying to figure out what to do with it. The ubiquitous little yellow notes (they now come in a variety of colors, but purists prefer the original yellow) are attached to nearly everything in every office. I especially appreciate the one on my computer screen that reminds me to back it up periodically. The FAX, easy to use, relatively inexpensive, and in every corner of the world is so much in use that AT&T estimated 88,000 faxes per minute were sent in 1993 in the U.S. That compares with a drop of 10,000,000 in the average number of pieces of business mail delivered by the post office since 1987.

Back to the Internet. The Information Superhighway is not new. It has been around and growing rapidly since the '80s. Although it was originally funded by the military for research, it is now growing on its own. Several million computers are linked around the world by high-speed data connections and tens of millions of users are accessing the computers and each other on the system. You can make a local call anywhere in San Miguel County with a computer modem and be on the net. You can use the network to send E-Mail (meaning Electronic Mail — people on the net call the other kind, the one with stamps, Snail-Mail). That's pretty good if you write a lot of letters, but most people use the phone or the fax. You can communicate on forums, with other people with the same interests. This can be good if you are in an obscure field and don't know anyone else in the neighborhood who shares your interest. There is everything from the Tiny Tim Fan Club to the Obscure Astrophysicists' Forum. The main skill that you need to do any of these things is the ability to type and to like to communicate with other people through a keyboard and screen.

If you really want to educate the next generation for the Information Superhighway, teach them to type. Instead of having schools worry about the nuances of today's computer interfaces to the Information Superhighway, they should be teaching typing.

None of it works without keyboard skills. The programs that get you there will change so radically each year, that you should only learn them if and when you need them.

Some years ago, the same kinds of people who are predicting that the Information Superhighway will change our lives were predicting that electronic banking would change our lives. Back then, we were supposed to have a future that would be lived in our electronic cottage. We would shop by phone and TV, order our groceries, pay our bills, take care of our business without ever leaving our homes.

I can't imagine why anyone bought that idea. Most summer weekends, people can't wait to get out, do things, visit friends, see other people. "Sorry, I can't go to the fireworks; I have to stay home and watch the home shopping network."

I used to write computer programs. It is solitary work and you interact all day with a keyboard, a screen, and a machine. You can't really explain the work to anyone that doesn't do it and you are generally in a room with no windows. People who stay programmers must like this environment. I didn't. Maybe that's why people who design computer networks think that everyone else would like to communicate the same way. I think that if we can't talk and if you don't have a Fax, I'll leave you a Post-It note on your door. It's somehow more personal than E-Mail and it costs a whole lot less.

July 6, 1994

⋆⟾⟸⋆

Is This the Party to Whom I am Speaking?

The phone company has just about finished upgrading all of the old lines in the Norwood area. Now everyone that has been struggling with a four party line can get a private line and everyone who has been waiting for several years for a phone can get one. With the new electronic switchboard you can get those extra services like 'call-waiting.' This is a feature that interrupts the call you are on with a new incoming call. It allows you to switch back and forth between two calls and be rude to both of them at the same time. There is also 'call-forwarding' which allows your calls to chase you around town and interrupt your friends while you visit them. They actually charge for those services. This is progress, I think.

While researching the population figures for last week's column, we came across statistics on the number of households with phones in the United States. There are approximately 95 million households and 93.9 percent of them have phones. That translates to the remarkable figure that 6.1 percent of 5,795,000 households don't have phones. Some of those are because they simply can't afford them or live in places where they can't get them, but there are a significant number of households above the median income with phone service available that choose not to have a phone. What a concept. No one calling to take a survey while you're having dinner. No one calling to sell you something while you are in the shower. No bill collectors, no tax collectors, no boring or irate people calling, ever. No answering machines, no phone bill, and best of all, no ringing shattering the peace of a Sunday afternoon.

For a small town weekly paper, we have a variety of unique personalities writing columns for us. We get our columns from them in a variety of unique ways. Except for the occasional fax, they don't come in by phone. Baxter Black generally mails a month's worth, each one typed on a different typewriter. I don't know how many typewriters or computers Baxter has, but he hasn't repeated one in the five months he's been sending us columns. Kate Lundahl delivers us her gardening column every Friday like clockwork, hand written on pink lined paper. Cynthia Zehm drops by on Fridays with a computer disk decorated with hand drawn stars on the label. We try not to read our horoscope until we print it on Wednesday. It wouldn't be fair to get a jump on everyone. Sheila Grother comes in on Sundays, if she isn't on an ambulance run, with her column and lots of pictures of weeds taking over the world. Although he's up and about now after his climbing fall, David Rote, our historian, would wheel in on his wheel chair with his column on Mondays. His computer is one of the original historic ones, and he hasn't changed the ribbon since 1985. It's kind of hard to read, but we usually manage to transcribe it anyway. Kirsten Anderson, our peripatetic food editor, says she can only write early Monday mornings. She usually wanders in with the column when she's not on a road trip. Lately the wandering has struck and this week's column was faxed from a casino in Laughlin, Nevada. Last week's was from the Grand Junction Hilton. Some weeks back it came from a Stuckey's somewhere on old Route 66. Carter Smith slips his column under the door on the way to the Lone Cone to watch Club Dance.

We do get two features via the new hi-tech world of telecommunications. We download the satellite map from the weather computer at the University of Illinois via the Internet. Their computer is state of the art and a lot bigger than our computer, but for two issues the phones have glitched every time we tried to download. The pictures came out striped and we couldn't use them. This is the second issue that happened, but fortunately this week, the editor's daughter had a very nice picture of a 4-H swimming party. We used it instead.

Our ferrier, Randy Sublett, practices the ancient profession of shaping hot metal to the feet of horses. He uses the Infozone in Telluride to send his column electronically through miles of wire to Golden and then back to Norwood. The phone company owns all that wire and generally we have to call each other several times to make sure everything is working.

Randy has a cellular phone, so I can usually find him. This time, when there was no column by Tuesday morning, I called and got the following recording. "Cannot connect due to invalid electronic serial number. Dial 611 for further information." I dialed 611. I got 911. The dispatcher thought I may have dialed wrong. We tried it again, same thing. I called the operator. They connected me with repair. Repair told me to call the operator. This operator told me to call Randy and tell him his electronic serial number was wrong. My wife drove to Telluride and picked up the column. I suggested to Randy that he get the pink lined paper that Kate uses and trade in his phone.

September 14, 1994

⊷⟫◐⟪⊶

Educational Television

After years of getting one-and-a-half channels on the tube, we bought one of those pizza pie sized digital satellite dishes a few weeks ago and joined the television age. We rationalized the purchase by telling ourselves that being in the news business, we couldn't live without *CNN Headline News*. Of course, we also hadn't seen any of the new dramas taking place in hospital emergency rooms or any of the new descendants of *Star Trek*. After a week we admitted the inevitable truth. With 200 channels, there still isn't anything to watch. And our reading has suffered.

Back in the infancy of television, Newton Minnow was head of the Federal Communications Commission. He surveyed the television scene and said, "Television is a vast wasteland." Well, Mr. Minnow, you turned out to be a master of understatement. Today, television is a vaster wasteland. Even the joys of watching CNN have been soured by the one-third of the program devoted to every belch of the participants in the murder trial in Los Angeles, whose name we have promised ourselves never to mention in print. As for the hospital dramas, it is hard to tell which operating room you are in, and the western channel doesn't show any John Wayne and the mystery channel never shows Alfred Hitchcock. Even with 200 channels there is precious little to watch. To be completely fair, there are some watering holes in the wasteland. Occasionally A&E has some fine programs, the Learning Channel has some excellent archeology and history, and you can find a lot about animals on Discovery. On the networks there is always *60 Minutes,* but Charles Kuralt is gone on Sunday mornings. Once in a while there is a good sitcom like *Grace Under Fire,* but usually Minnow's axiom holds up.

Trying to justify the purchase, we started looking for something different and came across a Canadian news network that shows half-hour segments of nightly news from world capitols. If they are not in English, there is a voice-over translation. You can find out what the Moscow or Madrid or London news thinks their countrymen will find interesting that evening. Based on the evening news you find that crime, disintegrating families, teenage pregnancies, oversized governments and deteriorating educational systems are perceived problems in many other countries, not just here.

There was a story on the German news coming from Bonn that was telling, with regard to personal freedoms. We have commented here before that the volumes of new government regulations emanating from Washington each year (70,000 pages last year) are severely impinging on personal freedoms. It could be worse. It seems that a stock swindler in Germany has been wanted by federal police for two years in connection with a swindle of over two-billion Deutsche marks. Even before the dollar's decline, that put him in a class with the biggest of American swindlers.

He and his wife eluded the German authorities and came to America. They rented a luxury apartment in Palm Beach, Florida and lived there for two years before he got a DUI, and subsequent checking found out that he was a fugitive.

The German commentator was incredulous that he could have lived openly in the U.S. for so long without being apprehended. He patiently explained to his audience how it was possible. "They don't have a registration law. Yes, it is true, there is no registration in the U.S. You can move or live wherever you want without government registration." There it was. We learned something. They *do* have a registration law. "Your papers please."

We told you it could be worse. Every time we think about what is wrong in America, we should remember that with all of its faults, our system is better than anything else that is out there. We need to work within it to make it better. There aren't any better alternatives on the other side of our borders.

Well, I guess there is some justification for the 200 channels. I think I will keep the dish a while longer. It is educational after all. Besides, Nickelodeon has reruns of *I Dream of Jeannie* all next week.

June 7, 1995

⊹⇒◉⇐⊹

Interactive Page Turning

Being so far from what some call civilization, putting out a weekly paper requires some degree of self-sufficiency. Although the type style you are reading is a font that is over a century old and the long narrow columns with fine lines between them have been copied from publications of the 19th century, and the eagle on our front page was originally drawn in 1870, we generate our paper electronically on sophisticated computers. The final product is printed on a classic newspaper web press using soy ink. There is a lot of hauling around of newspapers in this process, what with circulating in 3,000 square miles of one of the country's most thinly populated areas and mailing subscriptions to far away places.

Since the paper is already on computer, we could publish a computer edition and save all that traveling, not to mention a lot of newsprint. We won't. Last week we received a free copy of Encarta, Microsoft's electronic encyclopedia on CD-ROM. It is the modern way to learn. It is on CD-ROM and it is "interactive" and "multimedia." We were supposed to review it. If we compare it to other electronic encyclopedias, it is pretty good. If we compare it to a real encyclopedia, well, it isn't the same. Encarta is selling very well because interactive and multimedia are the buzzwords of our decade, but what do they mean, and do we want them in our homes? We'll start with multimedia. In the electronic jargon of our age, multimedia means a presentation that has sound, moving pictures and text. For some reason, a whole industry has grown up packaging sound bytes, text, and moving pictures in digital form on compact discs and they keep telling each other that they have created a new industry and a new way of teaching our children. It doesn't fly. Multimedia has been around since the first talking movies in the '30s. They combine text, motion and sound into a complete multimedia experience. Television takes it one better by bringing the multimedia show into the home. The CD-ROMs have very limited storage for

175

sound and motion pictures, and it will be some years before they can equal a good old Technicolor movie.

If watching multimedia on your television screen isn't generally educational, then why is watching it on your computer screen considered the modern way to learn? If you ask that question, the answer you get is "TV and movies aren't interactive." Just when we thought we had "multimedia" beat, along comes "interactive". Interactive means we can direct our research. We can just look at what interests us and skip everything else. We can click our mouse on the picture of Martin Luther King and hear the sound byte of "I Have a Dream" without ever reading the speech or having to put it into any kind of context. It is a kind of window shopping for information. Interactive encyclopedias are miles wide in their presentations, but only a few inches deep. Real encyclopedias are deep. They tell the stories that you need to put information in a context that will bring understanding. Flipping through the "H" volume of a paper and ink encyclopedia looking for "hamsters" might bring you to your first meeting with *Hamlet*. An interactive electronic encyclopedia would protect your children from this mistake.

U.S. sales of the Encyclopedia Britannica dropped from 117,000 sets in 1990 to 51,000 sets last year. Part of it is the expense. Starting at $1,500, it isn't an investment to be taken lightly. Besides, it used to be a status symbol to have four-and-a-half feet of Britannica on your bookshelves in the living room. Now the home computer has replaced it for status. The Britannica has over 44 million words. Computer encyclopedias have less than 8 million words. Maybe the sound and animation are important, and leaving out 36 million words is no big deal. There are some critics who say that it is impossible to make a comprehensive encyclopedia. There is simply too much information.

That is ridiculous. If anything, we need encyclopedias more than ever and they need to be as comprehensive as possible. To sacrifice depth of information for well-worn sound bytes and shaky animations is intellectually dishonest. Camille Paglia said, "It is intellectual laziness and post-modernist navel-gazing and just lack of IQ that would make any humanities people say,

'Oh, it's just impossible to have a general encyclopedia. We need *world* encyclopedias.'"

We'll keep printing on paper and using ink that doesn't come off on your fingers. We are going to confine our interactive learning to turning pages.

June 21, 1995

⋅→⇒◯⇐←⋅

Progress Was All Right. Only It Went on Too Long.

We borrowed our title from James Thurber. We aren't sure he was serious when he said it, but it fit our current mood. Having attempted to take a day off last week, we returned to the office and became immediately entangled in a seemingly endless roll of fax paper spewed out on the floor by the ubiquitous machine that was supposed to make life simpler. The answering machine had long since filled up and was endlessly bleating in an electronic voice with the timbre of elevator music, "You have 17 messages." Afraid to check our e-mail, we pressed the obscure codes necessary to check the messages on the cell phone and were greeted with static and alien voices informing us that the system was overloaded.

"We first shape our tools and then they shape us."

Having been multiplied by our machines, we now have to deal with input that goes far beyond the five immediate senses a million years of evolution have prepared us to parse.

Wait, you say, now you have the tools to deal with these intrusions. After all, we carry around a laptop computer, packing in its five-pound case more computing power than was available to a space capsule twenty years ago. After all, computers reduce our workload.

Does anyone believe that anymore? The futurist Alvin Toffler wrote a decade ago, "Making paper copies of anything is a primitive use of electronic word processing machines and violates their very spirit." He predicted, as did many other currently underemployed futurists, that we were entering a paperless society. It didn't work out that way. A generation ago paper was sold by the ream. That is, 500 sheets at a time. It is now sold by the 5,000 per case and a visit to Sam's Club or Office Depot will amply demonstrate only the smallest of companies buy but a single case. After all, the paper must be fed to the ravenous photocopiers, laser printers and fax machines simultaneously and, later, to cavernous filing cabinets, recycling boxes and paper shredders. Does anyone make carbon paper anymore?

Although there have been substantial gains in manufacturing output in the last decade through computerization and automation in the service sector so dependent on computers, the gains have been negligible. Investment per worker in advanced technology in the service sector rose by 116 percent in the '80s. According to the Federal Reserve and a Brookings Institute study, output per worker increased 2.5 percent during the same period. We feel in need of far more than 2.5 percent to answer those innumerable messages and deal with the yards of curling faxes.

The computer age brought some amazing typos to the front page of the Wall Street Journal last week. It seems that an editor relied on suggestions from his spell checker, which thought that attorney "Clyde Leff" was better referred to as "Cloyed Elf." Not to mention Georgine becoming "Georgian." Our spell checker consistently prefers Enter Net to Internet, but we usually resist the suggestion.

July 24, 1996

What, Me Worry?

Sometimes we have to tell ourselves stories. Humankind cannot bear too much reality.

T.S. Elliot

I woke in a cold sweat. The dream had been so vivid. I was below decks on the giant ship. The water was rushing in to fill the compartment. I was engulfed. The end was coming. There was no escape.

Now, why would I dream about drowning on an ocean liner when I lived 1,200 miles horizontally and two miles vertically from the nearest ocean? Get a grip. *Titanic* had claimed yet another victim.

There were real disasters that I should have been dreaming about. If my payment didn't arrive at an obscure post office box in Omaha in three days, my car insurance was going to be cancelled. My bank had left a message on my answering machine, and a yellow slip in my box announced a certified letter from Ogden, Utah. Here, I was having nightmares about a century-old shipwreck. At least the nightmare was distracting me from the real worry.

Fake worries are a staple of my self-treatment for anxiety. I grew up with backyard fallout shelters and Armageddon clocks. "End of the World On the Beach" stories were always at the Saturday matinees. Naturally, nuclear war was my distraction of choice.

I remember walking to school in the sixth grade. I had run out of excuses for the lateness of my report. It still wasn't done and I had lost the pictures carefully cut out of the *National Geographic*. Bright and warm, the sun broke through cloud cover behind me. I turned to look back, hoping against hope to see a mushroom cloud. A nuclear winter was far preferable to the wrath of the aptly named Miss Mudge, my teacher. I was bitterly disappointed.

Lest you think I'm alone in my lunacy, remember the story of the Millerites.

The Millerites were a communal sect living in upstate New York in the mid-nineteenth century. They believed the world would end in 1843. When the world didn't end on schedule, they called it "The Great Disappointment."

Without the world ending, they had to go back to worrying about thinning hair and thickening waistlines and overdue bills.

We are fortunate. There are so many more scenarios for disaster in the age of technology and special effects it is doubtful we can ever run out of distractions.

Nuclear Armageddon gave way to tidal waves in the *Poseidon Adventure,* and then capsized ships gave way to burning office towers in *The Towering Inferno.* Global warming and toxic waste created new conflagrations and even slimier monsters. The *Andromeda Strain* started us fearing the nasty little microbes all around us.

Now volcanoes appear on city streets and meteors surround the earth ready to destroy life-as-we-know-it without a moment's notice.

Even the vice president bought into the meteor scare and wants to spend significant new research dollars on destroying incoming meteors. It might even help his presidential aspirations, distracting the voters from his less than memorable vice-presidency. Besides, it would provide work for all those Star Wars defense scientists, unemployed since Reagan left office.

A whole new literature of food scares has grown up in the media. The dangerous-food-of-the-week stories have just about demonized anything that tastes sinful. It could be the start of a new Puritanism.

What will be our new distraction of choice, or will a real disaster come along to obviate our need for farfetched theories?

There was frightening news reported in the national press this week. Cocoa farms are declining, under siege from fungal diseases and ravenous insects. We may be facing rapidly escalating chocolate prices within two years and a worldwide shortage in five.

The prospect of a world without chocolate is too bleak to contemplate.

I was going to reconcile my bank statement this afternoon and try to figure out how to pay my bills, but how can I worry about these minor details while our cocoa trees wither in the field?

Winter 1998